The Tyran

Psychopolitics and Power

**To Adela Alemany Vila,
mother, artist and writer**

"I believe banking institutions are more dangerous to our liberties than standing armies. If the American people ever allow private banks to control the issuance of their currency, first by inflation, then by deflation, the banks and corporations that will grow up around these banks will deprive people of all property until their children wake up homeless on the continent their parents conquered. Emission power should be pulled out of the banks and restored to the people, to whom it belongs appropriately."

Thomas Jefferson. Letter to the Secretary of the American Treasure, Albert Gallatin, 1802-

Table of Contents

Page

Foreword	....	3
Chapter I. A Beautiful Spring Morning	....	7
Chapter II. Distant Visions	....	18
Chapter III. The Great European Migration	....	26
Chapter IV. An Image in the Mirror	....	32
Chapter V. A New Religion	....	42
Chapter VI. The Construction of the Great Story	....	51
Chapter VII. An Afternoon at Taif	....	72
Chapter VIII. Blurred Images	....	78
Chapter IX. Under the Microscope	....	84
Chapter X. A Formula for Success	....	98
Chapter XI. Stepping on the Accelerator	....	118
Chapter XII. Myths and Legends	....	133
Chapter XIII. Places of Obligatory Visit	....	145
Chapter XIV. Reviewing the Script	....	153
Chapter XV. A Repeated Scene	....	165
Chapter XVI. That Mysterious Character	....	173
Chapter XVII. What a Beautiful Landscape	....	179
Chapter XVIII. The Specialized Critics	....	190
Chapter XIX. A Genre of Fiction	....	214
Chapter XX. A Happy Ending?	....	221
Epilogue	....	220
Sources and References	....	239

Foreword

This book is the second installment of a self-imposed obligation. A close description, not exempt from assessment, of human evolution, which began with the publication of ´The Skin of God´. The reason for this small work is multiple. The history, practically in no occasion, does not represent an exact nor much less honest vision, of the real facts happened. Added to this, it is related from the watchtowers that hold a certain kind of power or only have the possibility to do so.

Accuracy, as a primary requirement, is at all times accompanied and therefore distorted by the interpretation of naked facts. And the valuation is always interested, or at least eroded. In the first part, we try to contemplate human evolution from its beginning to the present moment. This paper attempts to represent a necessarily superficial, but as broadly as possible, view of the social reality of the present moment, in its most relevant parameters. It therefore focuses on those factors that have an impact on the lives of individuals and groups. We will finish, with the third issue, which will mark as a goal, the projection of a medium-term future. To paraphrase an admired physicist, Neils Bohr, "predictions are always difficult, especially when they refer to the future".

Once ´what´ has been explained, we will try to explain ´why´, that is, the reasons for this work. There are several of them. Most of them refer to personal deformations. We do not know, nor do we want to, explain a certain phenomenon, without doing so from the beginning. The second reason has to do with the final objective, and at the same time, with another personal limitation.

We hate injustice, but even more, lies, understood as the adulteration of reality, with the express intention of leading to deception. Above all, as when it is the general rule, it comes from factual powers and is used in order to mislead and coerce the activity of the social majority. Unfortunately, continued lying has become the usual mode of message of the dominant elites, to the rest of society, regardless of nationality, race, religious creed, political orientation or activity.

It seems consistent with the foregoing motive, to explain the purpose or *'for what'*. Most of the world's population is being subjected, unauthorized, ignored and mistreated by an elite, numerically insignificant, but with a great deal of accumulated power. Power that is not authority. If this fact, as we explicitly affirm, has to be so, let it be so from the knowledge of the significant facts, that is to say, in an accepted and public way. We affirm that the ultimate motives of this situation are due -for scandal and recrimination of many- to the fact that the nature of the homo sapiens, of the human being, continues to be dominated by his basic instincts, and the so celebrated rationality, acquired in the evolutionary process, presents a double face.

The luminous part is directly responsible for progress. The dark counterpoint allows both its self-deception and the pejorative consideration of mass, a term commonly used by extractive elites to refer to all those who are considered different. We want each reader, as an individual, to be able to decide for himself whether or not to accept the conclusions and facts set out here, but with sufficient information to do so.

In the section of 'how' or the way to reach our objective, we continue to maintain the basic rules, already present in the first document and which will remain unchanged.

We have described the relevant facts, and some of them have been provided with an explanation. We have relied on the methodology and contents of traditional science, and on many occasions derived from a current theoretical orientation such as the ´sciences of complexity´ y of the ´complex systems theory´ in their different varieties, adaptive, evolutionary and on the verge of chaos.

The logic and philosophy of science, epistemology, as well as the scientific disciplines in use, especially anthropology, social psychology and sociology, have served as an explanatory framework and structural approach for the approach to reality. We have tried to maintain in the exposition, the necessary distance to the facts, required by impartiality and perspective as guarantor of objectivity.

We recognize, however, that in the points referring to injustice, especially poverty and within it, child poverty, it has been very difficult for us. We do not apologize to the reader for this circumstance, simply, understanding.

We have named most of the chapters, with titles from a hypothetical film aimed at the general public. This practice is due to the fact that, contemplated from a complete approach, in a zenithal shot, from above, as a professional filmmaker would do, the story told is almost totally similar to a Hollywood film. The genre of the film is easily identifiable. It is a tragicomedy. Likewise, as in the previous book, the dates are highlighted, for the sake of a greater ease of location of the facts or people, in the temporal continuum.

A desire, present from the beginning of the initial exposition and that we wish to maintain until the end. Facts have been described, potential explanations have been suggested, and judgments have also been made. But the conclusion, and also its use, is personal. Each one of the readers will value, interpret and add value to the panorama described here. If we manage to make the transfer from the author to the reader clear and useful, we will really feel satisfied.

Chapter I. A Beautiful Morning of Spring

A belief is not simply an idea that the mind possesses, it is an idea that possesses the mind.

- Roger Bolt. British writer and scriptwriter-

The month of November **1900** was lived as a splendid spring morning. The exuberant setting of Paris was the most appropriate for the Universal Exhibition, which marked the next entry into the new century. It would undoubtedly be an exciting period for humanity. Nearly **50** million people, visitors from all over the world, shared a vibrant, contagious, exciting and confident feeling, literally created by the relatively recent events of recent times.

The shared feeling was of a solid confidence in the future. And it appeared drawn with absolute clarity on the horizon. A clear future, sculpted with undeniable strength, that directed all humanity as a whole. There was no doubt that the future was projected in a single direction, forward and even its end, was also traced. It was by definition unlimited. Belief, the great theory of *´unlimited progress´* was strongly rooted on a world scale. There were enough reasons for it, all of them clear, demonstrable, objective.

Everything coincided, everything fit together. The great universal clock, the universe acted exactly, perfectly, repetitively and cyclically as Newton had demonstrated just a century and a half before. It was a perfect mechanism. *'Deus est machina'*. But this certainty alone was not surprising; society was governed by the same laws; fixed, repetitive, ferrous and immovable.

The **171** companies represented there exuded the same confidence and illusion. Undoubtedly, they would achieve an unimaginable expansion and consequently, the benefits that were assured by the demand of the growing market. They had all the elements to do so. The market was a solid existing reality, as was the physical universe, delineated in its confines and mechanisms by Adam Smith. Demand was an objective and testable reality. In short, trade had been perfected throughout its centuries of existence.

The growing commercial exchange, had found in the commercial company, its suitable formula; the risk assumed by the owners, was justly rewarded with the benefits and the support of the banks, created already in the previous century. The banks offered all the financial support necessary for their unquestionable and demanded expansion. But the economic facilities did not end there, incredibly. Three centuries earlier, another great support mechanism had begun to function for the newly-emerged company. The miracle of the *'stock Exchange'* created by the Company of the Dutch Indies. Progress was delineated as a new, almost magical way, an incredible miracle for the development of a world, which was in itself a perfect design; a divine gift, representing security.

But above all, it showed its best quality, the trait most valued by every human being, regardless of his condition: it was predictable. With a degree of success never imagined, it was susceptible to prediction, thanks to history and the recently emerged science. Of course, no one could have imagined the drift of the newly-emerging capitalist system adopted by the Western world.

Image of the main entrance to the Universal Exposition of Nations, held in Paris in 1900. It was attended by a total of 50 million people from all over the world, with 171 companies from the developed Western world also taking part.

Until the arrival of that moment, about a thousand years earlier, the fall of the Western Roman Empire marked the beginning of the Middle Ages. The seizure of Constantinople by the Turks ended with the cultural lighthouse that offered the ´Roman peace´ to all of Europe. Rome had provided the entire civilized world with a model of organization and, above all, a cultural reference.

The construction of communication routes -the Roman roads- and the supply of water, by means of aqueducts, baths and thermal baths, in short, a high level of development, although certainly, in the millennium that lasted the Roman separation between West and East, the empire had suffered a clear decadence.

In addition, Turkish domination had cut off the commercial flow established between the great Italian commercial centers -Genoa, Florence and Venice- with the Near and Far East. It was the first time in human history that development was undergoing an involution. The loss of cultural brightness led to the beginning of the dark age, the Middle Ages. Greek and Greek-Roman philosophy and culture lasted before the year **529**, when Emperor Justinian converted to Christianity, closing pagan schools, whose knowledge and tradition would be recovered and brought together by the Arabs.

The existing knowledge, in the form of orthodox and apocryphal writings, was accumulated in the libraries of monasteries and convents. The vision of the world acquired a theocentric format. God was the center of the whole universe, the architect of creation. The Christian Church, using this immense power, suffocated the population with religious pressure.

The era of religious persecution, witch-hunting and the Inquisition began. The coercion on the population was complemented with the imposition of feudalism as a political regime, sanctified by the Church. The feudal lords, imposed their power on the people, opposing at the same time, the authority of the monarch, of any monarch. With the incipient mercantilism cut off, agriculture became the necessarily prevailing economic model.

The inexorable rule of the existence of civilizations, change, began to operate also in this generalized situation. Between 1347 and 1352, there was a pandemic, the so-called black plague -bubonic plague- which affected practically all of Europe, the Middle East, China and India, mainly. More than 80% of the European population died, reducing the population to **20** million inhabitants.

Another of the defining events of the time took place in **1492**, in which the Genoese Christopher Columbus, with the financing provided by Isabel II of Spain, obtained the necessary economic resources, denied in Italy, to throw himself into the sea, in search of a new commercial route that would lead him to the East Indies. However, as is known, accidentally landed on the beaches of the Bahamas, in South America, although alternative versions, located the landing on the island of El Salvador.

After this discovery, the following Spanish discoveries would come from Pizarro and Hernán Cortés, to which would be added the Portuguese, French and English with William Drake -supported by the Queen of England, with the already famous Corsican patent- and also from the Dutch navigators, mainly. Thus began the great era of territorial colonialism, which still endures, with almost identical ways, ends and means.

In the cultural field, the great Michelangelo Buonarotti starred in a clarifying episode, driven by the sociocultural changes that had taken place in that historical period. He was commissioned by Pope Julius II to decorate the ceilings of the Sistine Chapel. This marvelous work, however, contemplated at present, does not obey totally, to the directives established by the Pope. Michelangelo represented religious history in a coherent and beautiful way.

But the most significant episode, in his way of working, refers to the method of chiselling, of possibly the best known sculpture in history, representing a human body: the David. Regardless of the fact that, in order to take advantage of the expensive block of marble on which it was made, he had to separate the left arm from the figure, the geometric proportions of the sculpture are mathematically perfect, revealing the knowledge of the golden proportions possessed by the Pythagorean philosophers. But above all, the deep study of human anatomy concludes in a majestic artistic concretion.

Along with him, other well-known artists such as Rafael Sanzio, Sandro Boticelli, Bramante and above all, Leonardo Da Vinci -supported by the Medici dynasty, thanks to his excellent gift for social relations as opposed to the sullen Michelangelo- are the origin of the return to classical Greek-Roman ideals. It was in the **15th** century and not before, when the beginning of the Renaissance could be located. This milestone will be key to the final establishment of liberal thought. A decisive limit for the social definition of the present moment.

Without trying to establish a concrete principle, to the generalization of the phenomenon of secularization of knowledge, that is, to the progressive return of interest -artistic in principle and philosophical afterwards- on the figure and human attributes, art and philosophy, they begin to develop the humanist movement, which will later become anthropomorphism, supported by the Renaissance tide, displacing the point of philosophical and cultural interest. God gives way to man, as the center of the Universe. It represents the passage from the theocentric vision to the anthropocentric vision of the Universe.

Successive contributions from outstanding scientists gradually and slowly shaped the breeding ground for rationalism and the coming scientism. Johannes Kepler's observations -using a telescope of his invention- extraordinarily exact, contributed to the anthropocentric vision of astronomy, defended by Nicolas Copérnico and Giordano Bruno- the latter, saved from the bonfire at the last moment-. Culminating in Galileo Galilei's contribution **(1564-1642)** to many, the true initiator of empirical science, although he certainly did not perform all the experiments he proclaimed, especially those concerning the fall of solid bodies thrown from the Tower of Pisa.

Isaac Newton was born in England, one day after Galileo's death. As it happened later with the other great physicist in history, Albert Einstein, using his brain as his main research instrument, published the laws of universal gravitation. When he pronounces his famous phrase "if I went that far it was because I rose above the men of giants", many have wanted to understand that he was not referring to the illustrious astrologers who preceded him, but rather to his Freemason coreligionists.

Certainly, he is considered one of the most outstanding great masters of the order, as well as an obsessive alchemist. He begins with his great discovery, the mechanistic movement, a current confirming the rationalism advocated by René Descartes **(1596-1650)**. Mechanism, through a process of osmosis or cultural generalization -also called expansive waves- will become the direct predecessor of the artificial construct of the market, assumed as reality and subject to the same laws, dominant in the universe and becoming an undeniable reality in the functioning of the commercial system.

The sociocultural panorama changed drastically in less than two centuries. Man became the center of the universe and reason, the valid instrument to analyze, describe and study, the relationship with nature, with reality. Metaphysics, the predominant specialty of the theological worldview, lost the battle as an object of knowledge, in spite of the influence of some isolated historical figures, although of great relevance, such as Thomas Aquinas.

Added to all this, Charles Darwin published his masterpiece, *´the origin of species´* **(1859)** in which he affirmed that, far from man's creation being due to any divine intervention, it was the law of natural selection, the force responsible for the survival of the strongest. The utilitarian morality, proper of the current savage capitalism, will find in this an invaluable collaborator, for the implementation of social Darwinism in economic performance, ethically justifying the supremacy of the privileged social classes. The survival and triumph of the strongest -fitness-.

The world -the universe- appeared as a great mechanism, precise, exact and predictable and this paradigm, could be applied licitly and by direct extrapolation, to any activity of human existence. On this basis, Adam Smith in his work *'The Wealth of Nations'* **(1776)** proposed a concept, the free market, as a regulatory mechanism of the economy. Subsequently, the system will be reaffirmed by the well-intentioned John Stuart Mill. The regulatory mechanism of the economy is, from this moment on, exact, self-sufficient and above all, self-regulated. Therefore, it does not need any adjustment, let alone external intervention, for its correct functioning.

Feudalism, as a system of social organization, declined. The power of the absolute monarchs was strengthened and one of the greatest and most relevant historical figures was formed, which last to the present day. The new historical figure of 'Nation-State' was configured with the fundamental purpose of protecting the different national economies and ensuring decisional sovereignty over their own wealth and economic processes.

It appeared, as a relevant representation that will extend into the future, with certain changes, of the bourgeoisie-the new rich who live in the bourgeoisie or city-and who will become the first capitalists, creating the incipient factories and above all, the manufacturing workshops, under more stable and rich monarchic states. As the financing needs of the factories increased, the first European banks emerged in the three main Italian republics, later extending to the most prosperous German cities.

Technology made its main contribution, with the invention of the steam engine by Watt **(1776)** giving rise to the second industrial revolution. Earlier, Gutenberg had invented the printing press **(1441)**.

Although the economic scenario was oriented towards Great Britain, it had the effect of a general phenomenon throughout Europe, reaching **50** million inhabitants, sponsored by the wealth derived from the commercial boom.

The French revolution, under the utopian motto of *'Liberty, Equality, Fraternity'*, opened the way to the century of lights, the eighteenth century. Here began the Modern Age and ended the high Middle Ages. The century of lights represented the ultimate detonator of individualism, as opposed to any other conception of man. In this scenario, in which the individual dominates nature and freedom, it is constituted as the maximum value, both at the philosophical level and in the social sphere.

Freedom from the state, geographical limitations and moral rules. The licit objective consists in the enjoyment of the earthly life, whose goods have the only sense of satisfaction of the new born individualism.

This is a general rule, in such a way that it originated the philosophical current of the single thought, in which the meta-theory of unlimited progress will become the immovable basis of liberalism and one of its basic principles *'laissez faire, laissez paser-* -to let go, let go- in its immovable and primary dogma, in the basis of the economic conception of neoliberalism.

In the economic sphere, and in this historical moment, two events must be highlighted fundamentally. The first of them, the evolution of the productive system towards a mercantilist modality or stage and later, transformed into incipient capitalism. Secondly, the creation of banks, with their subsequent transformation, in terms of functions and attributions.

Essentially, the triumph of rationalism as an ideological paradigm during the nineteenth century, the deeply mechanistic methodology of scientific procedure and the technological advance, derived from three industrial revolutions, constitute the basic ingredients for the appearance of the current model of globalized market, which rests as a theoretical element, in the implicit neoclassical ideal, concreted in the *'metatheory of ilimitated progress'*.

Chapter II. Distant Visions

> Chains only bind hands: it is the mind
> that makes men free or slaves.
>
> - Franz Grillparzer. Austrian writer and playwright -

The generic historical references in literature present, in their totality, an endogenous reductionism: they refer exclusively to Western civilization. Civilization, progress, technology, wealth and culture all focus on the paradigm of Western thought. The social system currently possessed by most Western societies is the direct result of a costly struggle led by different groups that are undervalued or ignored by the ruling class. Universal suffrage and the class struggle itself, May **1968** in France or the Bolshevik revolution, are some historical examples. However, this only responds to a partial reality.

The different religions, races, women themselves, the mentally ill, the physically handicapped, homosexuals, workers and the poor, have constituted groups, slowly and progressively recognized by the leading leaderships of Western societies -though not exclusively- in the slow evolution towards modernity.

With exactitude, the general model of structuring modern societies corresponds to the combination of two formats prevailing in antiquity. The first of them, arises with the Egyptian civilization, that began to form, approximately, **3000** years to. C.

The figure that held the primacy, and therefore, placed at the top of the command structure, was the Pharaoh, considered as in most civilizations of the time, half God, half ruler.

The central organizational feature is that, for the first time, a division of labor is instituted through the use of separate caste criteria. The principle of division of labour will later be used as the basis for the formulation of the classical theories of sociology. The main areas of stratification of the collectivity are represented by the priesthood, the scribes or administrative and the army, sometimes commanded by the pharaoh himself. The population was constituted by slaves and workers, who received a salary -consisting of a small amount of salt- as payment for their work.

Both groups were in charge of carrying out the great works, the megalithic constructions, among which the pyramids stand out, dedicated to the honor and eternal rest of the governing gods. Among the caste of specialists, there were the doctors -basically climbers- and the artists -either painters or goldsmiths- who were responsible for the decoration of the temples.

The pyramids were mostly constructions that housed tombs of pharaohs and representatives of the highest castes of Egyptian society. Their purpose was Eminently religious. However, the pyramids built according to exact mathematical proportions, represent the pyramidal structure proper to the social distribution and power emanating from divine authority.

The second civilization, which has profoundly and permanently influenced advanced societies, has been the Greek civilization. It has offered subsequent generations decisive achievements among which it is worth highlighting, philosophy, politics - with various concrete formulas, such as dialectics or oratory but mainly, democracy as a format of social government. Organized in independent city-states, it recognized, however, its belonging to a common culture -Greek or Hellenic culture-. The maximum value was the polis -city- and with independence of stages and cities, that were governed by kings, the senate, was the organ of discussion and elaboration of the norms of coexistence. Politics, as an essential activity, begins at this historical moment.

Greek civilization is a milestone of decisive influence on the development of human civilization. The consideration of the human being as a full member of society, concretized in the polis or city, determines a political activity that pursues the common good as the main objective through the establishment of democracy or power of the people for the people.

The Roman civilization would be the direct temporary heir of the Greek civilization, making new and fundamental contributions to the development of societies. Its system of civil architecture, such as roads, public baths, irrigation systems and urban waste canalization, represented a notable advance in the infrastructure of modern cities. Recreational spaces, such as circuses and auditoriums, were a source of distraction for its capital, Rome, which reached a population of probably more than **1.5** million.

The great Egyptian constructions had a religious purpose. The enormous pyramids, constituted the refuge for the transit of the spirit of the great governors to the territories of the gods. However, their pyramidal form constituted an exact geometric representation of the prevailing world view in the Egyptian world, more specifically of the embodiment of power. At the top, divine power, shared with the monarch.

A tradition extended and practiced in the ancient civilizations of Central and South America; the god king. The transmission of power is rooted in an untouchable metaphysical principle, the divine will. Unquestionable by someone who does not belong to the privileged class. The transmission belt continues descending, first towards the monarch and later towards the aristocracy and the privileged castes. And at that very moment, it is cut abruptly.

After the period of time corresponding to the low middle age, the European peoples followed an undisputed path, towards unity under the form of monarchic government. The scientific and cultural revolutions have established pillars, more and more emphatically, in the construction of advanced societies, facing the avalanche of demographic growth and its ordering, within a governable system. Here is the central question of social development.

The scientific disciplines oriented to the study of man and his social grouping, have broken down the phenomenon of life in collectivity, in society, uninterruptedly, especially sociology. Similarly, the sciences that shift the focus towards individual action, such as psychology or anthropology.

Individual differences constitute a fortunate fact, described and explained by different sciences. A qualitatively different question arises with the constitution and valuation of social groups and classes. The **11** European countries that use the monarchy, in any of its modalities as a form of government, constitute the greatest historical representatives of imperialism.

The motives for this practice of conquest are purely economic; the justification, however, is religious; the evangelism of the conquered peoples, as a safeguard for salvation and the abandonment of pagan practices. The historical outcome concludes with the extermination of the autochthonous cultures, in short, the elimination of difference. An illustrative example comes from the colonization of America, both in its central part and in the entire southern cone.

The loss of the religious connotation of the monarchy does not modify its sociological significance. The affiliation of an individual to a social group, also at present, only takes place by means of two parameters; the right of birth or the level of disposable income. In the case of the two social classes most representative of the privilege, the monarchy and the aristocracy, they walk unfailingly united. The bourgeoisie, which has constituted the historical germ of the capitalist system, has had a different conception and formation. Capitalism has been in history a key approach and practice in social and, above all, economic development.

A fact that has been confirmed, until the confluence of a series of factors that will determine its meaning and pervert its principles, starting the contemporary panorama. Western societies today have used some pure forms and others combined, the monarchy as a form of government. The absolute monarchy and the parliamentary monarchy are the most common. But in all of them, the oligarchy continues to function as the real engine in the exercise of real power. Democracy, as Plato announced, has perverted itself, reducing itself to a representative democracy and moving away from the participatory option.

This premise has produced a large number of sociological contributions. Historically, all societies have been strongly hierarchical and divided into classes or castes. The question about the real cause of this phenomenon inevitably arises. In essence, nothing distinguishes the current pyramidal configuration from the tribe or animal herd. Certainly, today's societies incorporate democratic principles, coming from Greek civilization. But they are more akin to cosmetic measures, aimed at complacency and at obtaining ease of government, than to the real implantation of their underlying philosophical principles.

Democracy becomes an isolated and convenient act for the definition of a type of government. An irrefutable argument, when in reality, it is totally opposed to the Greek spirit. It was not intended to be a pure nominal exercise, but rather, on the contrary, a real mode of social dynamics. In other words, we were not looking for a representative democracy, we were trying to achieve a participatory democracy, in fact, a way of understanding the social collective. The rulers considered themselves mere managers of the real power that emanates from the people.

Today, managers, using a business simile, consider themselves more shareholders entitled to capital dividends than mere executors. Great historical achievements, such as universal suffrage, have resulted in simple fallacies, becoming blurred caricatures of their initial essence.

The equality defended by ideological tendencies, political parties, numerous organizations and opinion prescribers, results from a concept with a legal and philosophical base. National differences have been constructed and disseminated on the basis of the possibility of escalation and social progress of the individual in the social structure of a country.

This is precisely the essence and social motto of American society, later inherited by Australian culture. A clear example of the long list of fables erected in postmodern history. The scarcity of means and resources continues to strangle the less favored classes, under the false and offensive pretext of overpopulation and the scarcity of resources and means. Pure neoliberal doctrine.

The concept of power is one of the defining pillars of the social structure. Society, in its geometric drawing, is an asymmetrical figure. Power, transmuted into structures of control and government, ends in a coercive culture. The different mechanisms of authoritarian exercise are manifested in each of the spheres of action of the social individual.

Chapter III. The Great European Migration

"Man is born free, responsible and without excuses."

- Jean Paul Sartre. French philosopher and writer-

A third factor to consider, in the historical journey towards the formation of the model of hegemonic capitalism, led by the United States of America -USA-, is found in the great European migrations, especially after the second industrial revolution, from the year **1750**. The migratory phenomenon has undoubtedly made possible the formation of the first world economy of the last century. This same migration, which at the moment rejects the European Union, relieved in its responsibilities of government in the past, by the forced march, although relatively voluntary, of more than **60** million Europeans towards the new continent, if you count the migration of the beginning of the last century.

The Industrial Revolution centered primary economic development in Great Britain. The textile industry developed considerably. The application of the machine to industrial production, not only significantly increased productivity, but in reality, meant a high point in industrial development, as it provided the possibility of accumulating energy for the first time, throughout human history. The process of industrialization, originated a general demographic phenomenon and present at any time and place, consisting of the population migration, of the agrarian zones to the great urban concentrations.

A second phase of this wave of concentration involves emigration, in search of other horizons in which to progress and find work and well-being. In the case of old Europe, between **1700** and **1850**, the greatest migration in human history begins. In a first wave, European citizens from the countries of central and northern Europe, the United Kingdom, Germany, Ireland, Sweden or Norway left for the United States and Canada.

In the last third of the 19th century, Europeans from the countries of southern and eastern Europe, especially Italy, Spain, Portugal, Poland and the Russian Empire, joined. These extended the migratory space also covering the central and southern areas of America, mainly Argentina and Brazil.

The beginnings of industrialization in North America, a practically unpopulated continent, offered multiple investment and work opportunities to the population of central and northern Europe, the first to be affected by industrialization processes. The typical phases of industrial mechanics were replicated in the New World.

In **1850**, the first railway networks and communication routes were installed, the basis of any commercial development. They clearly constituted the priority object of concern for the new government. When, at the end of the **19th** century, South America was integrated into the international trade system, specializing in the export of agricultural products, the labour supply expanded, acting as a visible magnet, which attracted the population of southern Europe, which at that time was initiating the process of economic modernization.

Many groups and individuals have migrated involuntarily, like the millions of African slaves. Nevertheless, European immigrants fought the great war that culminated in American independence, concretized in the signing of the Declaration of Independence.

One of the mental baggage carried by European emigrants was the inherited culture, including belonging to hermetic societies, which had proliferated in the European rationalist period and some of them would either replicate or arise exclusively in the United States of America.

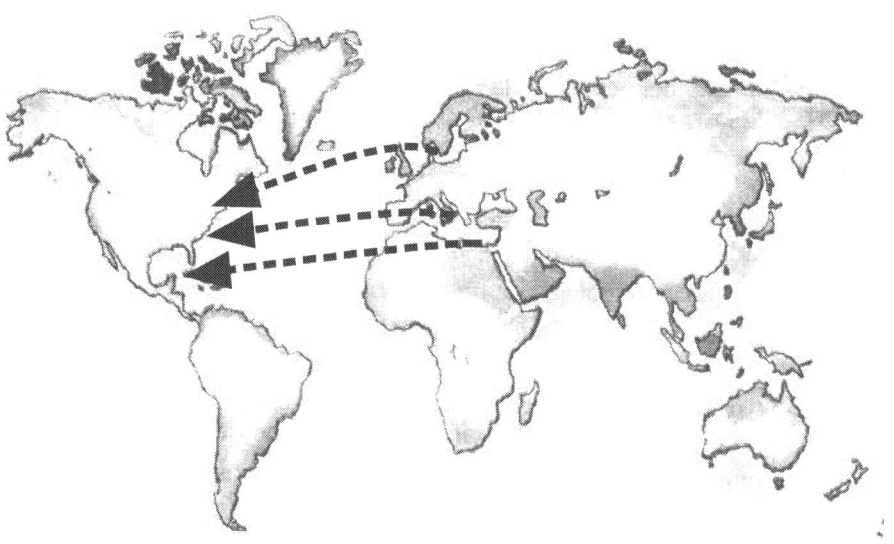

Migration from the old continent to the American continent has been a historical constant. The promise of new unexplored lands and the desire for a dignified and better life have made possible the human energy necessary for the conversion of a new nation into the economic and cultural leader of today's global world, leading the so-called model of savage hegemonic capitalism.

The European migration towards the American States actually became the desired American dream. The law of the 'New Lands' in the continuous push of the whites towards the West of the country, segregating in reserves the original Indian population, was accompanied by the main promise of colonialism, consisting in that all that new settler that conquers a parcel of land, would possess it, without any other rule or legal obstacle.

The promise worked as expected and the expansion towards the immense west began and did not stop in the conquest of the land. Immediately, it was followed by the gold rush. Indeed, America was the promised land, the place where dreams were fulfilled, that desired space, where wealth was possible.

Until the moment when, like every dream, it ended up languishing, due to the continuous abuses and transgressions of an economic system erected on false theoretical premises and even more, by the deformation of the abusive practices inherent to stock exchange capitalism.

The communities of British, Polish, Latin origin, especially Italian and Central European, faced the task, once the civil war was over, of building a model country from scratch. An option that has not existed in Europe. In this way, a highly contradictory social configuration was once again shaped in history. USA -United States of America- probably represents the most advanced democracy in the world.

Based on the application of logical principles of action, they have managed to shape the most complete and effective study and work programs in the civilized world. The effectiveness in the areas of coordination of the multiple public rooms of a federal state are truly admirable.

The most powerful multinational companies emerge there. A federation has been formed that functions effectively. In the face of all this, they certainly lead the world's highest levels of corruption, at least from a relative perspective.

Public, legal and security bodies hold global standards of corruption. The police and the judiciary lend themselves to bribery by drug traffickers and large transnational corporations. Lobbies, or parliamentary depression groups, are an invaluable tool of coercion. The fundamental difference with other countries is that the taxpayer's money is the object of great respect, saving the destination of reserved funds of the government, a significant percentage of taxes.

Its destiny, the political and armed intervention of the nation that considers itself, in a self-attributed way, the police of the world. However, the publication in the media of a public figure's misconduct means his professional death automatically, in any area or specialty.

In addition to this, and having starred on behalf of Edgard H. Hoover and the FBI, the most scandalous ´witch hunt´ in the history of civilization, only comparable to that starred by the Spanish Inquisition, has a highly developed capacity for self-criticism. The film director, Oliver Stone and many others, are a good example. Obviously, American culture does not represent a model to imitate. **40** million people, despite the efforts of the administration of former President Obama, -through his Obama Care program- remain without medical care. But this statement is also relative.

Nevertheless, it stands as a country option, preferable to other current alternatives. Here and in this historical moment, the first attempt of confusion between two concepts took place, which had been handled as interchangeable, when in fact, they were not interchangeable at all. The basic concepts of liberalism were fixed, with the constitutive guidelines of neoliberalism, totally and absolutely opposed.

Liberalism represents a set of beliefs, after the French revolution, defender of individual freedom from power, as the philosopher's stone of his system, thus becoming the indestructible basis on which to build a state, based on law and justice. It is a belief, a philosophy of life and, at the same time, a worldview.

Neoliberalism, on the contrary, uses arguments specific to liberalism, with the objective of justifying an action exclusively centered on the economic area. A practice, fundamentally egocentric and presided over by material greed. It is a reductionist approach, interested and oriented to the use and accumulation of individual property, without any consideration towards the rights of the other.

While liberal philosophy protects the rights of others, insofar as this element guarantees its own, before the law and justice, the neoliberals justify the accumulation of possessions, with absolute independence and contempt of the other, under the perverse justification of individual rights.

This conception will originate, one of the components of the justifying base, together with the utilitarian ethics, of the neoliberal ideology. In short, at this precise historical moment, ideological political liberalism and purely economic neoliberalism are juxtaposed.

Chapter IV. An Image in the Mirror

> "I proclaim aloud the freedom of thought and let all those who do not think like me die."
>
> - Voltaire, French philosopher and writer-

Hipatia of Alexandria was murdered publicly, during the decadence of the western Roman Empire. The main motive was not political or even economic. She was a professor of the illustrious academy of philosophy. Her desire to know and her curiosity indirectly ended her life. If Hipatia had had an organization to protect her or at least help her, her destiny would have been very different.

The concealment of secrets from the prevailing power or exclusive knowledge, from the rest of the population, has been the historically fundamental motivation for the appearance, existence and durability of hermetic societies. At the present time, they continue to constitute an inseparable instrument of the financial practices of the international capitalist elite.

The term hermetic, in the etymological sense, comes from Hermes Trimegistus, a Greek deity, commonly used by ancient alchemists in their secret practices. The confusion existing between sects, secret societies and hermetic societies, is understandable since they extend to ancient history and are confused in their interests and objectives, power and public notoriety and in their very different degrees of organization.

The usual motivations for belonging to a sect, such as the search for identity, protection, adherence to a particular worldview or religious realization, are not typical of hermetic societies. There are methods to clarify the dense variety of alternative organizations. The first of them obeys to the understanding of the oldest and most common historical mechanism, object of its existence.

On the contrary, an example of a sect is represented by the famous "murderers", more precisely, the hashishies or *Hashis Eaters*, who were born in Persia in the eleventh century, for purely warlike purposes. Some organizations, though real, have been mitigated as to their motivations, evil traits, or scope in their plans through fiction or legend. Certainly, there existed the Templars, the Priory of Sion and the Illuminatti. As it is known, the Templars were originally a military order.

Their main objective is to protect the pilgrims on their long march towards the Holy Land of Jerusalem. The probable discovery of wealth - some believe that it constituted the legendary treasure of King David, gave rise to their subsequent economic power, which spread throughout Europe, becoming bankers of courts and kings. This accumulation of power was indisputably the cause of its extermination of all its conclaves simultaneously, ordered on the same day -apparently on a Friday the thirteenth- by Pope Clement V. The subsequent flight of some of its members, their concealment and possible survival in the population of *Esenios*, is historically questionable.

The Priory of Sion has been the object of countless legends and distortions. In spite of written and visual documents, which affirm its ancient birth and permanence in time, a renaissance seems to be possible in the present Paris, specifically in **1957**.

Originally, they have been attributed the permanent care of the lineage of Jesus of Nazareth, the holy grail -appeared in the novel 'The Da Vinci Code' by Dan Brown-, as well as the protagonism of his old plans, directed towards the formation of a world government, which would carry out the subjugation of the human race. The reality seems to indicate, rather, a modern attempt at profit, based on an ancient belief.

The search for wealth and the utopian attainment of immortality originated the grouping of the first alchemists. The chimerical pretension of obtaining through the treatment of metals, the conversion to gold and therefore, wealth, was originally the search for the philosopher's stone. But in reality, the ultimate purpose of the authentic alchemists was the achievement of immortality. They sought the combination of elements that would allow them to merge with the infinite and permanent cosmos, to transmute into pure energy, to eternalize. This was the concrete origin of the objective existence of the Illuminatti, is found on the contrary, historically documented, as well as their confrontation with the orthodox church, once they were object of attack on the part of the religious organization.

Identified in their origin with 'Bavaria Illuminated'. This society, originally formed by enlightened, scientists, writers and intellectuals -illuminated, instructed-, had as its primary objective the protection of its members against external attacks and the production of cultural and scientific communication, through the exchange of knowledge between its members. Likewise, the same myth regarding the search for submission of the known world has fallen on this organization.

However, the archetype of a society that is hermetic by influence and extension, not without a certain mythical halo, is Freemasonry. Formed in the late Middle Ages, as an authentic professional guild -"franc maison" means noble house, large house- and made up of builders and specialized construction workers, it was perfectly structured, according to the degrees of master, officer and apprentice.

The installation of the norm or degree of ´*Freemason accepted*´ became the key and reason for its great expansion. Numerous members of other orders, sects and lodges, join the society. Progressively but inexorably, their initial profile has undergone substantial modifications. Intellectuals of different kinds and economically affluent subjects, progressively profiled an organization with objectives of greater political, intellectual and more pragmatic and broad ends.

Influenced by social events, the different lodges, at a given moment, became business meetings or social congregations. However, the existence of a solid programming, ritualization and internal organization, has led them to become one of the largest global organizations, which now has more than 6 million members. Rosicrucians. At the height of the Lutheran Reformation, in Germany, an unknown character, known as Studion, appealed to all the alchemists of the world and in Nuremberg, founded the order of the Rose and the Cross.

The Bohemian Forest, one of the most representative images of hermetic societies. Founded in San Francisco in 1872, the Society has counted among its members personalities belonging to the socioeconomic elites such as Franklin D. Roosevelt, David Rockefeller, Robert Kennedy or Bill Clinton.

These guilds gradually became societies faithful to general ideals such as fraternity, equality, and peace, and their meetings became more social events than business meetings. Four or more of these guilds, called lodges, united in London on June 24, **1717**, to form a general lodge for London and Westminster, which, in less than six years, became the Grand Lodge of England. This organ represents the general lodge *'mother'* of the Masons in the world, and from it they have derived all the important and recognized lodges of the present time.

The ´Big Lodge of All England´, was formed in York in the year **1725**, that of Ireland in June of the same year, and that of Scotland in **1736**. The York section was placed under the jurisdiction of the ´Grand Lodge of London´ at the end of the 18th century.

As a result of the patronage of the order by members of the nobility, the rising British bourgeois class regarded Freemasonry as a means of social success, and as a result, the order gained popularity. Masonic ideals, based on religious tolerance and the fundamental equality of all people, harmonized with the growing spirit of liberalism during the **18th** century.

Another of the basic principles of Masonic orders, throughout the English-speaking world, has defended that religion represents an exclusive matter pertaining to the decision of the individual sphere. Historically, the Roman church has opposed the existence of the order. Opposition to Freemason societies has followed two directions. The first of these, of a religious sense, was that manifested by the Catholic Church, although Freemasonry does not exclude Catholics.

In fact, a large number of them belong to lodges, especially in South America. The second level of opposition is clearly political. During the decade following the **1821** kidnapping in Batavia, United States, of William Morgan, a Mason member who had threatened to publish his secrets, a general protest movement emerged in the eastern and central states of the United States. In the northern states, the Antimason Party was created, which was erected for some years, practically the only opposition to the current Democratic Party.

The newly created Antimason Party appointed a lawyer, William Wirt, in **1832** as its presidential candidate, but was defeated by Andrew Jackson, declared a supporter of Freemasonry. From that moment on, Freemasonry encountered little political opposition in the United States and practically no other country. This scenario underwent a radical change with the coming to power of National Socialism in Germany in **1933.**

In that same year, Hitler made the Masons responsible for various subversive activities, including all the incidents that led to World War II. He decreed the dissolution of all Masonic associations in Germany. Among the notable members of Freemasonry are composer Wolfgang Amadeus Mozart -whose opera The Magic Flute- revolves around the Masonic ritual - and writer Liev Tolstói, whose novel ´*War and Peace*´ extolled the ideals of fraternity advocated by Freemasons.

Representative image of Freemasonry. The quadrant and compass refer to the great work of God in the creation of the world. They also identify the beginning of the specialists of the construction of the Middle Ages, the master builders and the division of the professional degrees including the officers and apprentices that would automatically become levels of belonging to the Masonic lodge.

In Spain, where the Spanish Civil War **(1936-1939)** had not yet ended, **1,000** people were considered suspected of belonging to the Masonic movement, and in **1940**, the ´*Law of Repression of Masonry and the Communism*´ were promulgated, retroactively to the year 1934, declaring the affiliation to a Masonic lodge to be a crime. Subsequently, a list of 80,000 suspects of belonging to Masonic lodges was established.

The grouping of global financial elites into hermetic societies is a core requirement for the understanding of their most elementary feelings and their form of sociopolitical behavior. The basic forms of individual relationship, predominant in the total collective, are based on a characteristic behavior. The ´cronyism´ and the ´clientelism´, originate as direct derivatives of their worldview and ideology, in which they occupy a prominent role, their own individuality, their aspirations and the need for support and recognition of those whom the typical neoliberal considers their equals. The second general condition requires the perception and situation of privilege, a common feature of belonging to hermetic societies.

The term, ´privilege´, derived from Latin, refers to the legal conditions of that which is considered private, of the exclusive field of particularity. This feeling of ownership becomes an element of comparison with the rest of people, those who are of different class, those who are outside; the others. It fits and combines perfectly with the neoliberal personality archetype.

Belonging to a secret group, and in most cases to several of them, provides considerable competency support with respect to other potentially competitive groups in the domain of the relevant business areas, and of course, in the design and implementation of policies aimed at defense and supremacy, of individual values and interests, both economic and legislative.

Members of hermetic societies are, by definition, personally and socially influential, and today's hermetic societies have lost any trait of religious mysticism. Likewise, their meetings and calendars have become public, but not so, the content of the debates and agreements, although evidently they refer to the economic, social and political agenda of the globalized world.

Chapter V. A New Religion

> "Freedom has no value in itself, you have to appreciate it for the things you get with it."
>
> - Ramiro de Maeztu, Spanish Writer-

The emergence of a dominant elite in the long historical past has a number of general features in common. But unfailingly, at the top of the scale of these conditions is the conception of the other, the different or different subject. Curiously, this fact has been the cornerstone of human evolution; it was the ray that illuminated the development of the species. On the basis of the existence of the other, always different, abstract thought and language developed. The survival of the tribe and then of the village was based on the union of forces and on the need of all the individuals that conformed it.

The second characteristic common to the elites is not a direct consequence of their own actions. It requires the confluence, with greater or lesser presence of chance, of certain historical and/or social coincidences or vectors. In the case of the first homo sapiens, the bonanza of a sufficient period of time to allow their evolution and subsequent concentration in large cities. The third indispensable factor necessarily rests on the disposition of a coercive or violent means, which has normally been exercised by armies. A philosophical or at least ideological conception is chosen or created to justify the actions undertaken. Sometimes it is of a religious nature or has part of its components. In other words, religion is only used as a platform of support and cover for a given vision of reality.

But in any elite and at any moment, the objective is identical: the possession of absolute power over others. The power supported in the dominion of the economic, vital or strategic springs.

The neoliberal ideology is immersed in an experiential duality. While in the metaphysical plane, any of the religions professed by its members prescribes an attitude of mercy and help to any needy individual, in the social sphere, has consolidated in practice, a new cultural materialism, in which the new God, the supreme icon and maximum expression of doctrine, is called accumulation of wealth.

Marx proposed a social analysis, dialectical materialism, because his primary argument highlighted the relevance of economic rules, and especially the means of production, as generators of social classes. Today's society, dominated by neoliberal ideology, has enshrined cultural materialism as a conceptual framework for social behavior.

The dominant materialism has been classified like *'schismogenetic'* because it also involves an automatic division of citizens, and their grouping into differentiated classes. It results in a binocular vision of society. A conception, representative and director of the single thought model. Simplistic, reductive, selfish and curiously, with a notable dose of unhealthy and recalcitrant idealism.

The rest of the factors necessary for the permanence of the religious fact, continue unalterable and present in the culture of materialism. The presumption of the authenticity of their own belief, fanaticism in the defense of their ideological pillars and fervor in the apostleship and teaching of supposedly absolute truths, which are often not understood by the social majority.

The reverential fear of everything that continues to be a mystery - mysterium-, that overwhelms or impacts -tremendum- and that attracts irretrievably -fascinans-, are basic components of an ideology that, because it has been adulterated, has become a pseudo-religious belief.

The appearance of the current dominant financial elite brings together, as could not be otherwise, all the components described. The triggering historical circumstance is anchored in the triumph of liberal thought, propitiated by the emergence of the rationalist paradigm, definitively consecrated by the French revolution. From that point on, neoliberal thought is based on a logical fallacy. It reduces and adapts the liberal philosophical principles, extolled by the rational conception of man and consecrated by the Enlightenment, only to economic action. Individual freedom stands as a supreme principle and against any principle of authority.

From there, the defense of the defining protagonism of the individual initiative, against the normative attempts of the different western governments. It pursues the ideological premise, represented in a single sentence containing: Minimum state, maximum individual initiative, more graphically expressed, the achievement of ´minimal State´.

The neoliberal crusade rebels against any attempt at regulation. It defends the nonexistence of frontiers, advocates the deregulation of goods and, above all, capital. The symbolic component is revealed as a fundamental support. Its creed: God, Homeland and Home. Money, suffers a transmutation in its role of incentive or means to obtain wealth.

The means becomes an end in itself. It becomes the indispensable lubricant for greasing the inexorable machine of power. Two basic premises emerge within the neoliberal economic conception. First, maximization will require the construction of a global, total market. This principle is indispensable, in order to understand the functioning of the neoliberal model. The productive units, the volume of supply, the markets and above all, and this principle is a priority, the margin of economic profit, must be maximized.

The second guiding principle, standardization, consists in obtaining an optimum of uniformity, to the point of allowing the replicability and substitution of machines and people, which will germinate decisively in the international division of labor. A doubling of the geography at the scale of the company, as suppliers of raw materials, in a complementary way, others that provide the production or labor, and finally, the rest, who assume the banking function, safeguarding the economic surplus or profits safe from contingencies through the creation of tax havens. Above them all, as an indisputable reign, consumption, or better consumerism; the design of a global and compulsive consumer market.

Thirdly, and as a logical consequence of its extractive intentionality, there is a principle that has become a generalized model, as well as a methodology of action. It is about the socialization of losses and the privatization of profits. The economic activities related to the coverage of primary social needs, such as education, health care, energy or food, are mainly identified with potential profit. In its belief, the world must be individual and private. The state is not only unfit to intervene, but rather morally and economically unfit, according to its conception of reality.

The same process of transformation is applied to its temporal component. Utilitarianism is object of a qualitative conceptual transformation, almost offensive. The principles declared by the classic utilitarianism, promulgated an undeniable principle of the human conduct. Jeremy Bentham **(1748-1832)**, enunciates the principle that every human being tends towards obtaining everything that produces pleasure. It was, in origin, a theory on human motivation. But it is John Stuart Mill **(1806-1873)**, the author of the conceptual conversion and the application of this maxim to economic behavior.

According to the economic discourse, it established the conclusion that if all individuals pursued the maximum satisfaction of their needs, through the laws of the free market, the end of the chain, resulted in an enrichment of the social whole, and therefore, in the general welfare.

The combined logic of the principle of absolute freedom with transformed utilitarianism leads to the distorted principle, now ethically justified, of the total freedom of maximalist trade. The result is a hyperbolic objective: maximum profit in the shortest possible time.

The choice for the benefits of the free market as a system obeys a philosophical conception, in human reality, of the meaning of all that is beyond the line of one's own individuality. Two consequences of the application of the principles of action described, are the consideration of the damage generated to the majority of the world population and to nature. The consequences in both cases are logical consequences of the system and therefore irrelevant.

The first, they, is originated by the intrinsic conception of capitalism. The second factor, the consideration of nature as a supplier of resources, at the same time that as a container of industrial waste, has been originated, mainly by the excessive productivism.

Both perversions are considered and thus labelled as externalities of the system. A system that should not be forgotten is legitimized by science, according to its prostituted consideration.

This premise necessarily implies contempt or at least the underestimation of those elements. In the productivist equation of neoliberal thought, both concepts -the individual and the environment- would be considered an invariant, that is, a variable that always remains the same, that is not considered relevant and therefore, is not introduced into the economic equation. In purely economic terms, they are considered part of the capital. In other words, land, labor and capital are infinite and, of course, interchangeable.

It is mainly for this reason, because of the philosophical and human consideration of the other, that the elites need the support of their peers, the others who think and act like themselves and their grouping in small groups, totally separated from the others, for their mutual assertiveness. There is still another possible simpler explanation for the dominant behavior: persistence or better, preponderance of the animal instinct. The strongest individual dominates the herd. The triumph over his fellows, at the moment he has achieved power, allows privileged access to reproduction, food and territory. In short, when the dominant individual holds the power, he feels satisfied.

The bases of the established order, denominated by social theorists and political scientists like *'hegemonic wild capitalism'*, is established with the leadership of the USA, geographic center of the second industrial revolution and place, in which the use of electrical energy, wireless telegraphy and the railroad is generalized. To do so, it will need the reproduction of one of its basic supporting elements, hermetic societies. As a clear example, one of the best known, Skulls & Bones to which presidents of the nation, bankers, politicians and many other influential people have belonged.

Another indispensable piece, in the implementation of the neocapitalist economic model, has consisted of resorting to a specific business philosophy. In this case, starring the so-called *'School of Chicago'* that Milton Friedman led in his economic discipline. The monetarist approach to the economy, in full confrontation with Joseph Maynard Keynes and with a large number of economists who defend interventionist policies, develops the theory *'accionalista'* of human behavior.

Probably, because the suburbs of Chicago constitute a privileged field of observation of the poor and uprooted masses, this theoretical current substantially affirms that there is nothing predetermined in the conduct and that the individual shapes his future and makes his decisions through his own actions. The religious argument of free will thus obtains a more than dubious academic confirmation. The contemplation of the world panorama and of one's own evolution up to the present seems to agree with these ideological approaches.

The uncomfortable assertion of the coincidence of behavior, its variability and its instinctive tendency, which we have previously formulated, is annoying and even offensive to average minds.

Moreover, it seems to deny the verifiable evidence of altruistic behavior, which promotes humanitarian aid actions and campaigns, without which the disadvantaged masses would perish or disappear. Fortunately, there is no such contradiction. The variability and diversity of human behavior, both individual and group, contemplates and promotes behaviors of solidarity and social support. Again in the philosophical area, the conception of the static order prevails, that is, the intended solution of the problem here and now, alluding to concepts, purely artificial, nominalist and justifying, such as the general welfare.

From the sustainable development movement, basic concepts such as inter-generational equity have been highlighted, with the objective of ensuring the optional welfare of future generations. This is a new concept that neoliberal ideology does not want to confront, as many others do, that entail changes in attitudes or habits of conduct, especially in substantive areas.

There are different nouns for neoliberal ideology: conservatives, fixers, continuists, reactionaries, creationists, reductionists, mechanicists, simplists and many others. Neoliberal thinking transfers all the responsibility and the consequences generated to the system chosen as the economic model, the free market economy, supported by the false logic of the *'utilitarian ethic'*.

The free market is the only option, since, in imitation of physical systems, it is governed by verifiable and, above all, manageable laws. The inherent undesirable consequences, such as poverty and generated inequality, are cataloged through the usual strategy represented by the use of euphemisms. They are called like 'systems´s externalities' or, in their most serious cases, *'collateral damage'*.

Other justifications come from the Thomistic philosophy of Saint Thomas Aquinas, with Aristotelian roots, such as the established natural order or a more modern concept, derived from evolutionary theory, the survival of the strongest individual -fitness-, known in terms of political sociology as ´Darwinism´. Basically, both conceptions, religious belief and social worldview, are interconnected. There is an unfortunate confusion between religion, morality and ethics, which is invisible to the neoliberal mentality. Economics replaces ethics. In this way, responsibility towards others -the true meaning of ethics- automatically disappears.

The objective fact is obviated, that the model used as a market structure is merely an extrapolation of a complex macroscopic structure, deterministic by definition and subject to physical laws, under normal, immutable conditions. The physical universe is not reflected in the social scenario. The social configuration and within it, the economic activity, results from a decision of the set of individuals. At this point, rests all the effort required to advocate and sacrifice the neoliberal economic model, mainly led by world political leaders.

Chapter VI. The Construction of the Great Story

> "The worst truth costs only a great displeasure.
> The best lie costs a lot of small disappointments
> and in the end, a big disappointment."
>
> Jacinto Benavente. Spanish playwright-

The **nineteenth** century had witnessed profound changes in socioeconomic topography throughout the world. At that time, a critical milestone was reached to understand the current situation and the events that occurred in the international economic configuration. The central banks acquire the capacity to mint bank money, with the commitment of the state, from exchange to real currency, in theory, to facilitate international payment.

The conversion of the bourgeoisie into the nascent capitalism propitiated the appearance of a legal figure that, like any innovation, has represented both a facilitator and a means of economic fraud: the legal person. Thus arose the corporations, financed by the banks and the stock exchange, the latter created for this purpose. The States also required financing, which is why they facilitated the emergence of central banks. England **(1667)**, Spain **(1782)** and France **(1800)** were the first countries to design this new financial figure. At the same time, new services and instruments were created in order to facilitate commercial exchange.

The bill of exchange and industrial banking emerged. The banking figure diversified into commercial and fixed business, according to convenience and opportunity. In France and Germany, credit institutions, corporations, which provide long-term loans that could be exchanged for shares of client companies, emerged.

The economic boom spread to the productive sectors, which were also driven by technological innovations. Transport was developed, including steam navigation, as elements of infrastructure and communication, a basic condition for economic exchange. New materials -iron and steel- were incorporated into the productive process and the use of hydraulic energy was extended. Industrialism was generalized as a form of production and capitalism as an economic model. In the United States, both federal and national banks acquired the power to issue currency and charge interest on debt. A profitable business.

At that time, according to data from the Carnegie Institute, **1 %** of companies accounted for **44 %** of world production. The concentration of capital and oversupply had begun. The imbalances of world trade produced the emergence of the first poor countries, such as Russia, Portugal or Japan, at the same time as the development of new colonies, in the image and likeness of the old Europe, such as Canada, South Africa, Australia or New Zealand.

The imperialism of past times became legalized colonialism. The colonial distribution of the world, suffered a drastic turn, at the end of the Second World War. Prior to the armed confrontation, 10 countries controlled the whole world, according to the agreement promulgated in the ´Berlin Conference´ **(1885)**. European imperialism was imitated by the Russians and Turks, led by the pressure groups prevailing at the time; Church and Army.

The acquisition of new territories facilitated the implantation of several key factors for the progressive generalization of neoliberal thought. During this period, the international division of labor and production factors took place. Parallel to the course of capitalist implantation, the national and international legislative power configured norms and laws, inevitably directed to the protection of the international capitalist system.

In addition to this, at that time, the banks began to issue paper money, over and above their reserve capacity -the currency they keep in their safe- based on the principle of the federal reserve: only a part of the **10 %** of the demandable capital needs to be available in the safe, based on the fact that, under normal conditions, all clients and creditors would not request that their accounts be liquidated at the same time. If that were the case, the feared one would be produced and known ´corralito´ -playpen-, as it happened in Argentina.

The excess of banknotes issued allowed the banks to grant more credit, which increased the speed of currency circulation, improving the balance of the banks and the general monetary system, all artificially. Between the years **1815** to **1913**, the monetary offer multiplied by **20**, while the real or metallic money only made them by 4, the rest was bank money, that is to say, there was a clear undue issue of currency. Banknotes multiplied by 14 and sight deposits by more than **50**.

At the beginning of the First World War, the sum of gold and silver did not reach **15 %** of the international monetary set. It should therefore be stressed that the primary objective of large international banks, which is at the basis of economic profits, lies in the concept, generation and management of the methodology of ´debt´, both nationally and internationally.

The recognition of the national debt implies obligations of an economic nature, subject to the vagaries of international capital, such as the fixing of the interest rate, which is managed in such a way that the initial debt can never be canceled. Secondly, it imposes moral dependencies. It takes on the formal aspect of an attitude of concession and willingness to cooperate. In short, it makes possible the submission of national, institutional, business, social and, of course, individual units.

The international monetary system is streamlined with the mechanism of total compensation between banking entities, that is, the debtor companies or institutions pay the creditors periodically, including this procedural requirement to the entire banking system -clearing-. This requirement increases its effectiveness, logically, the greater the volume. In this way, money does not move and is replaced by electronic accounting entries.

Thus, in essence, the recently appeared bill of exchange was a payment order, issued by the borrower against the debtor in favor of a bank -beneficiary- in which the borrower had a credit account. The bank collected and paid the bills for and against a particular customer, and granted a credit or overdraft limit, up to a certain amount, in which the bills receivable exceeded the bills payable. The arbitration band regulated the parity between squares or countries and currencies. The real result is that the dreaded and venerated balance of payments is, in reality, a constant flow of electronic accounting entries. That's all.

The great depression of the New York stock exchange in **1929** represented -in this case, yes- the first serious setback to the recently instituted financial capitalism. It became a pressing need, the reconstruction of a new market mechanism, according to the logic of liberal thought.

Bretton Woods is a small, quiet town in the state of New Hampshire in the United States. At the Mount Washington Hotel, between June 1 and 22 of **1944,** a year before the end of the Second World War -the greatest human holocaust in history with a number of casualties that the most optimistic estimates put at 60 million dead- a meeting was convened of the Monetary and Financial la *'Monetary and Financial Conference of the USA'*. In it, the bases of the new world economy would be established. At least in appearance, the need for these agreements was based on the conviction that similar reasons that had provoked the war could be reproduced, in case of not regulating a free market economic policy, at world level.

In the financial and power circles it was considered that the peace after the 'Gran Guerra', would force the labour market to absorb a huge number of soldiers, with the risk of a new depression, similar in magnitude to the one experienced during the 1930s'. For this reason, the United States, together with England, was working on the idea of a great post-war agreement that would offer guarantees of prosperity and development to the entire world. Certainly, it was already known at that time that the allied forces could not lose the war. The United States was building military weapons, four times larger in volume, than those that could be destroyed by the German army, in the worst imaginable scenario.

A large representation of **44** countries, all of them belonging to the first world, attended the meeting. The third world countries, both Asian and African, were in many cases still colonies of the old European empires. This fact would mark the subsequent events, above all, the so-called oil crises that would begin in the **70's**. A very broad representation was present.

The conference was attended by the United States, England, France, China -which would withdraw five years later, after the triumph of the communist revolution- and the Latin American countries, which would later fall victim to the production model defined there. The Soviet Union and the countries of its influence participated in the meeting, but did not adhere to the agreements.

The new international economic order, born of the Bretton Woods agreements, was based on an international monetary system, which initially adopted the gold standard for the convertibility and support of different national currencies. In these agreements, the United States undertook to maintain the price of gold at $35 per ounce, allowing the purchase and sale of the reference metal at that price, in an unlimited manner.

Therefore, the price of the dollar remained fixed, which assumed the monetary leadership of reference in world trade. The rest of the countries established the price of their currencies in relation to the American dollar, committing themselves to intervene in the currency markets, so that these would be maintained in a fluctuation band with respect to the dollar of **± 1%**.

The Bretton Woods agreements contemplated the creation of the *'International Monetary Found'* -IMF- and *'World Bank'* -BM-, initially called *'International Bank for Reconstruction and Development'*. In this meeting, the amount of the deposits and the quota assigned to each participating country were established. The weight of each member's vote was determined based on the share of funds contributed by each state. The IMF was created for the sole purpose of lending working capital to member countries with balance-of-payments deficits in exchange for agreements aimed at reorienting their economic policy. The World Bank, on the other hand, was in charge of financing the apocalypse originated by the Second World War.

In addition, The ´GATT´ -the English acronym for the General Agreement on Tariffs and Trade, the embryo of the current World *World Trade Organization´* -WTO- was created. This agreement operated with periodic meetings of the member states, in which negotiations tended to reduce tariffs, according to the principle of reciprocity. The negotiations were carried out in a format of individualized consideration, that is, member by member and product by product, using the presentation of petitions from each country, accompanied by the corresponding individual offers.

Along with the global financial structure, was created in **1947**, the Intelligence ´Central Americana´ -CIA-, which would assume the role of information provider, to the complete financial system, designed for the dominance of the global market. The ´General Agreement on Business and Trade Rates´ was initially signed by **23** countries, including Australia, Belgium, Burma, Brazil, Canada, Ceylon, Chile, China, Cuba, France, India, Lebanon, Luxembourg, the Netherlands, New Zealand, Norway, Pakistan, the Czechoslovak Republic, South Rhodesia, Syria, South Africa, the United Kingdom and the United States of America.

The members of the agreement would have successive meetings, with the objective of improving its regulation and functioning. The contracting parties that founded the WTO officially terminated the terms of the "GATT 1947" agreement on December 31 of **1995**, although the United States of America (U.S.A.) had to resolve, at the same time, at the internal level, the consequences originated by the great depression of **1929**, known as the black Thursday.

In the decade of the **30's**, the overcoming of the precariousness that characterized the North American economic situation provoked confrontations between Congress and the Executive. There was a real conflict, to decide the appropriate measure to increase trade promotion and stimulation of employment. The Congress approved, at the request of Franklin Delano Roosevelt -the president at that time- an interventionist policy, in accordance with the doctrine of Joseph Maynard Keynes, by means of the principles exposed in his reference work 'la General Theory of the Occupation and the Interest of Money'(1936). Under the name of 'new deal' -new agreement- **(1933-1938)**, it was considered a necessary measure to overcome the profound national economic crisis.

It institutionalized the legitimization of the role of the State in the economic stabilization and in the generation of full occupation as an objective. This measure became the central theme of the economic debate in those historical moments, just as it is today. It is basically the substitution of the economic practice of budgetary orthodoxy. State expenditure is used with the criterion of punctual convenience. The ultimate purpose consists mainly and almost exclusively in maintaining employment and therefore economic and social stability at times of declining private demand for labour.

State intervention thus attenuates economic cycles. That is to say, the State can act as a decisive element in economic behavior, through the use of annual budgets, even if indebtedness is generated by the investments that are considered necessary, in order to safeguard economic well-being. Thirty years later, the United States went through a new situation of economic asphyxiation, originated by the expenses derived from the Vietnam War.

At the end of the decade of the **60's,** the amount of American currencies, held by foreign countries, hamstrung the convertibility of the dollar. It was suspended in 1971 by President Richard Nixon, through the signing of a provision of law to that end. It is worth noting that, like many other unpopular economic measures, it was not widely publicized. From this moment on, a delicate balance of a balance of payments system between all the countries that make up the world economy is set in motion. This new configuration of trade made it possible, after the end of the Second World War, to implement 'Plan Marshall', aimed at the reconstruction of the European market -European Recovery Program-.

The USSR, together with Poland and Czechoslovakia, renounced to participate, while the *'Economic Organization for the Economic Cooperation'*, precursor of the current OECD -Organization for Economic Development and Trade-, received **13,000** million dollars at that time.

In Europe, the main recipient of aid, the operation of loans followed a clearly established mechanism. The European companies proposed reasonable purchasing actions, which if approved by their government and later by the OECE (European Organization for Economic Cooperation), whose primary mission consisted of estimating the needs of each country, avoiding duplication and distribution of aid, passed to the commission of the plan, which purchased the requested products, normally from North American companies. The American salesman charged his country for the Marshall plan. Instead, the buyer paid his government, thus avoiding the outflow of foreign exchange. Half of the adjustment went to Great Britain and France, ⅓ part to Germany, Italy and Holland, and the remaining third to the rest of countries.

The results were spectacular. There was an important increase in occupation and production, on the other hand the plan favored economic growth forcing the dismantling of the control of production and markets, restoring the stability of prices and exchanges.

Until **1958**, European currencies were not convertible to dollars. In **1951**, France and Germany created a supranational body, *´European Community for Coal and Steal´* -CECA- for the joint management of these two basic products. Belgium, Italy, Holland, Luxembourg and Italy were quickly incorporated into the set of countries that would form the initial nucleus of the *´Economic European Economic Community´*, called in its early years ´European Common Market´, currently la ´European Union´. The global response to this initiative consisted in the formation of different monetary unions, especially in Latin America, with the Latin American *´Association of Integration´* (ALADI) and MERCOSUR and the *´Economic System for Latin American Economic and the Caribe´* (SELA). For their part, the communist countries formed COMECON.

Without needing to detail, the international payment system used different modalities, depending on the due date. According to liberal logic, the monetary system is the way in which the currency is organized within a country or internationally. The currency can be real or fiduciary. The latter term makes direct reference to la *´faith´* o the creditor's conviction that the debtor will satisfy the debt, in the same way that at present, the acceptance of any banknote is trusted, with the only guarantee of the signature of the president of the corresponding central bank, since it does not have any real value. The theoretical function of the international monetary system consists of ordering the foreign exchange market and stabilizing it. Basically, it helps to equalize the balance of payments and facilitates access to international credits.

That is, on the one hand, it regulates the granting of credits, on the other, the compensation of the fixed parity of the dollar with the different currencies, mainly with the yen, the pound, the franc and the framework. It begins with this great logistical operation, a long sequence of economic and social fables that have marked global behavior. The first and greatest phantom of national, corporate and individual behavior can be found in the spurious term ´debt´. Development loans constitute one of the gigantic and most deceptive shadows of the spider's web, woven by the international monetary system, and perfectly explain some of the behavior of current governments in their obsessive and ineffective reactions to economic changes.

The mirage generation mechanism of ´International Debt´es simple in its apparent logic, and criminal in its essence. The granting of a development loan to any country, by the IMF, entails, in addition to the credit conditions of amount, interest rate and renewal -specifically of an economic and financial nature-, the commitment on the part of the borrower to comply with a deficit objective, previously established unilaterally by the concessionary entity of the credit.

The International Monetary Fund, in short, fixes the degree of deficit of the countries to which development loans have been granted. In other words, practically the entire world. The different governments of the debtor countries are responsible for the fulfillment of the commitment thus established. The national deficit includes the various items of national accounting, which incorporates government investment or expenditure. They are mainly public investments and, above all, expenditure dedicated to the preservation of social guarantees and rights.

These items are therefore controlled and fixed by economic entities, whose right rests on economic indebtedness. In other words, it is the International Monetary Fund, which is responsible for setting the budget of any debtor country in the areas of education, health, unemployment coverage, dependency or research and development. The incredulous reader can carefully review the Spanish case in the last legislatures.

This category of public expenditure includes pensions, attention to marginal groups at risk of exclusion and subsidiary coverage, such as unemployment. In short, those expenses, which during more than **200** years of civil and labor struggle, have become the so-called ´welfare state´. Consequently, in the event of non-compliance with the deficit, as has occurred at some point in time, by European and South American countries, or practically all of the countries in the world, it will be necessary to take into account the fact that the deficit has not been met. the IMF, demands that this initial condition be fulfilled. One of the ways of doing this is obviously through budget cuts in national investments in the social area.

The global consequences of the implementation of the Marshall Plan after the Second World War are divided into four distinct periods. The first, called the ´*golden age of capitalism*´ **(1950-1973)**, has represented the period of greatest historical growth of the economy. It was characterized by strong global and geographically differentiated growth. GDP growth in the advanced countries, mainly in the OECD, tripled that of previous years and doubled that of later periods. Growth experienced a strong acceleration in the rest of the world and cyclical fluctuations were mild and inflation moderate, but with a strong acceleration in the following years. It ends precisely in the same year in which the first oil crisis occurs, caused by the increase in prices by OPEC -*Organization of Oil Producing Countries*-.

Growth follows simple rules, in reality. The most backward countries at the beginning of the process and the countries losing the war, experienced greater growth than the rest. This is the case of Japan, Germany and Italy. The second group includes the Mediterranean countries, Spain, Greece and Portugal. In this period, the most advanced countries tend to reach the income levels of leading countries such as the USA -catching up-. So, in **1973**, the year that marks the end of the period of growth, due to the appearance of the oil crisis, the industrialized countries had very similar incomes, ranging from **61 %** of Italy to **73%** of France, with respect to the USA. By 1990, the convergence ratio had increased even further, ranging from **71 %** in Italy to **82 %** in Japan. Another characteristic of this period is the extension of industrialization to the backward countries, especially the Mediterranean countries, Eastern Europe and the Far East.

Debt as the first link in the great story, the first coercive figure in the financial system, materializes in the feared spectrum of international debt. It is a complex problem. On the one hand, the developed economies do not grow enough, not to cancel the debt, but not even to compensate for the interest generated by it. Secondly, in a space dominated by a common currency, such as the euro zone, monetarist policies do not act the same in all economies, nor do they produce the same effects, since the different nations have different structural compositions.

This is the case of Germany, the United Kingdom, Italy, Spain or the Nordic countries. For example, Germany, with an unemployment rate of around **6.5 %**, requires, according to classical economic logic, solutions totally opposed to Spain's need, with a structural unemployment rate of over **20 %**.

Structural and therefore historic. The automatic question arises as to whether, at any time and under any special circumstances, any country in the world has managed to pay this revolutionary tax, already institutionalized by the global world. The answer is obvious.

Never, in all recent history, has any country in the world canceled its initial debt. What's more, in the case of Ecuador, its president Rafael Correa, decided to audit the debt and not assume that part he considered unjust or abusive. He kept his promises. There was no sanction of any kind by the International Monetary Fund, nor penalization of the rest of the world's institutions.

Since **1973**, the year of the first oil crisis, caused by the control of price and production by the *'Organization of Petroleum Exporting Countries'* -OPEP-, only China, India and Japan have experienced real growth until **1990**. The latter has firmly committed itself to the guiding principle of the second technological revolution, based on science and which makes the country the best technologically prepared competitor -fitness-. However, despite the effectiveness and objectivity of this general principle, which has been repeatedly and constantly demonstrated, there are other strategic options for the development of a country as a whole. For example, Spain opts for a model of ´sun and beach´, la ´austericide politic´ and the strongest monitoring of the cutback in investment, suffocating and reductive, dictated by the *'Troika'* -International Monetary Fund, World Trade Organization and World Bank-, strictly applied by the European Union -EU-.

At the risk of being repetitive in the exposition of essential ideas on the definition of the desired country model, the main action of any effective State in the economic scenario is totally contrary to the current neoliberal policy. State intervention in the economy takes place with two fundamental objectives.

The first, by means of public investments, directed towards the creation of employment, associated with large infrastructures. The second acts fundamentally through the implementation of social welfare policies.

These policies are aimed at improving the quality of life of the population, providing a minimum of income to people unable to obtain them directly and also aimed at making it possible for all to have access to goods and services, previously reserved for the powerful classes, especially in the field of health and education. Favorable policies are promoted to maintain employment in the face of falling private demand in crisis times.

The most visible fundamental aspects of the welfare state focus on social security (pensions, retirement, orphanhood, widowhood, incapacity for work and unemployment), free health care and the generalization of free or subsidized general education. These policies generate significant economic benefits in the medium and long term. Investment in research and technology policies and programs brings medium-term market opportunities, creates previously non-existent jobs and, in short, generates wealth by contributing to the national economic balance, i.e. to the increase in gross domestic product and, consequently, to economic growth. In addition to this, advances in social policies help to achieve a healthier, stronger and more motivated human capital.

In this way, the benefits of the welfare state have been financed, increasing the taxes and trying to make their distribution more equitable. To this end, state revenues do not come so much from indirect taxes, but from taxes on income and wealth and on company profits. In addition, these taxes are subject to progressive tariffs, so that higher profits correspond to a higher tax rate. The purpose of these measures was to modify the distribution of income, i.e. to use the income from the highest tax rates, corresponding to the richest segments of the population, in order to finance services for the most disadvantaged groups. A progressive imposition measure, in which the State complemented, by means of a tax scale, the salary that workers obtained from companies, while at the same time offering greater security in situations of unemployment for unexpected reasons, such as invalidity or accidents at work.

In this way, families that depended on wage income could devote a greater proportion of their income to consumption, money that, moreover, common sense advised saving, in order to face difficult times, now partly covered by social benefits. Despite the criticism of these policies, the redistribution of income was minimal. The Spanish worker pays **50 %** of his salary among all the taxes required, that is, he works for his compatriots, half of his annual working time. However, the percentage destined for the redistribution of wealth was **0.34%** according to data from **2015**.

In spite of that, the social coverage, constitutes indisputably, the greater cost of the items of the national accounting, reflected in the general budgets of the state. The economies of the second half of the twentieth century are characterized by the decisive intervention of the State in the markets, regulating and stimulating them. In the name of the community, the State assumes the obligation to make one of the fundamental economic choices: the distribution of resources between present and future uses. This duality, based both on the functioning of the free market and the intervention of the state, is called the mixed economy.

It would be an ideally advisable combination. However, the real decision-making bodies are located in the global financial powers, owners of the international debt. Thus, inevitably, the historical confrontation of the weak against the oppressor arises. The use of power as an instrument of vital oppression.

In the case of the European zone, recently, Iceland, a country of **300,000** inhabitants, was forced by the EU to rescue its three main banks, with a cost per citizen of 12,000 euros. The government, supported by the population, refused outright. There were never any consequences. It should also be remembered that called *´German miracle´*, after the Second World War, was made possible thanks to the cancellation of **50 %** of the public debt, at that time for an amount of **50,000** million euros. Moved to the current figures, an amount equivalent to a quarter of the Spanish gross domestic product.

Finally, some members of the European Union do not share the common currency. This is the case, of course, of the United Kingdom, but also of some of the admired Scandinavian countries, which serve as a reference and model of advanced social development, leaders of European social democracy, such as Norway and Sweden.

The neoliberal principles, currently questioned, are based on the primacy in the world economy of the ´monetary policy´. They have been historically defended by Friedrich Hayek **(1899-1992)**, and later by Milton Friedman **(1912-2006)**, visible head of the so-called *´Chicago School´*. On the opposite side, the classical market position, personalized in Joseph Maynard Keynes **(1883-1946)**, advising control, through state intervention. Keneth Galbraith **(1908-2006)**, is one of the last and most recognized representatives of this position.

The decade of the **80's´**, made coincide in time, two of the hardest and fiercest representatives of the neoliberal position, in the Anglo-American axis, for the umpteenth time. Ronald Reagan in the United States and Margareth Thatcher in the United Kingdom.

The American president, Bill Clinton, has exemplified, like few others, how to adopt the philosophy of ´pendulum´ The iron defenses of the neoliberal position have led to the present moment, especially after the fall of the Berlin Wall in **1989**, ending the utopia of the centralized economy of the URSS.

At present, the main representative in Europe of the austerity strategies recommended by the economic Troika is Angela Merkel, who has adopted one of the emblematic phrases of neoliberalism to justify her policy: "there is no other option". The countries of Latin America, perhaps with the sole exception of Brazil, have suffered interventionist pressure from the United States. The Arab countries, mainly, but not only, of the Persian Gulf, have been the object of the second phase of the ´North American Imperialism´, ´militarization´, in a continuous way since the **90's ´**, mainly.

A simple observation of the distribution and number of U.S. military bases in the Gulf area, in order to protect oil reserves, explicitly evidences the situation.

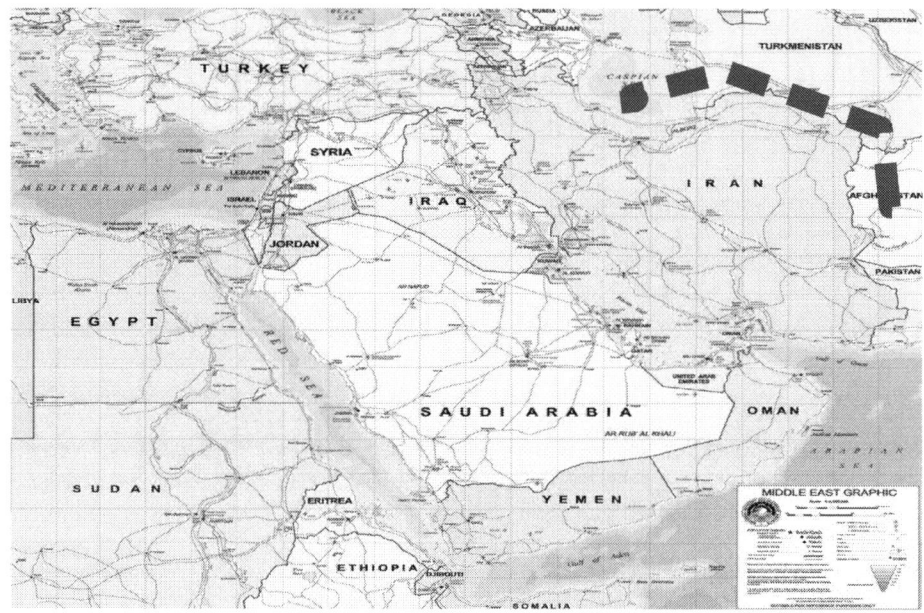

The American military bases in the Persian Gulf establish a strong military line, represented by a red line, against the former communist enemy with the intention of preserving the flow of oil that represented 43% of the world production of crude oil.

The *'imperialism'*, is not at all, a movement or behavior of the human past. Today, it continues to show identical phases and methodology. The beginning consists of an interference in the economy of any relevant country, directed frontally to the exploitation and extraction of national wealth. Secondly, the advertising, sometimes with a propaganda tint, of neo-capitalist principles and models. This is the phase of *'cultural conversion'*. Third, when the unfounded threat or importance of the case requires it, resort to *'armed intervention'*.

Militarization, in fact, constitutes the third phase of imperialism. One slogan has been in the media in recent years: "There has never been an invasion in a country where there is a Mc Donalds". Illustrative and coherent.

The basic question, then, does not focus on deciding between one or another model of action. The neoliberal, monetarist conception allows the maintenance of ´control´ world economic. Any other option represents the loss of power. It is a possibility of such implications and terrifying magnitude, which becomes an unthinkable option for the control mechanisms of international capitalism. For this reason, the generalized strategy consists of implanting an ineffective present as a vaccine against an uncertain future.

The neoliberal creed has implanted a characteristic behavior in the world, which it considers its legitimate field of action. All the countries of South America, with the only exception of Brazil, have served as its field of experimentation, starting with Chile and ending with Argentina. The formula of inter-country relations is limited to the heavy implementation of a well-designed model of imperialism. It repeats incessantly the formula of cultural imperialism.

They are relentlessly seeking the signing of economic treaties on the free circulation of capital and goods, as well as the total deregulation of the markets. The North American multinational companies find themselves ready and ready for the extraction or transformation of the natural wealth of the Latin countries, the Venezuelan oil and gas, the tin, rubber and iron of Bolivia, the Chilean copper, the coal, copper, gold, silver and zinc of Argentina, the emeralds of Colombia. Africa, has followed the same path, with the Coltan of the Congo, the gold of Ghana and the South African diamonds. In a second phase, it logically seeks the implementation of government regimes, prone to neoliberal ideology, mainly dictatorships or presidents with ideological connection. The American Intelligence Central -CIA-, has collaborated actively and effectively, in that phase of North American imperialism.

The basic philosophy of neocapitalism is therefore fundamentally extractive. This fact is reflected in the weakened African, Caribbean and Asian countries.

Far from global cooperation, for multinational capital groups, the economy remains, and perhaps more than ever, a zero-sum game. One of the participants must lose to allow the profit of the most powerful player. In this case, the triumph entails the annihilation of the weakest, and in this way, the accumulation of profit is obtained. The application of the dominant principle of profit maximization takes care of the rest. The weaker opponent, in this permanent and repetitive game, is subdued and, in most cases, disqualified.

The use of existing niches of economic resources and their management become an unavoidable and fundamental objective for international capitalism. In addition to the natural resources, mainly fossil fuels and minerals necessary for global hyperproduction, there are other sources of economic benefits. One of the historical sectors with the greatest potential for generating economic surpluses is used: the arms industry. Of the approximately **200** local or regional armed conflicts counted after the Second World War, none of the participating countries or factions were arms producers. All of them have been acquired from the producing countries.

Thirdly, and although it may seem so initially, the destruction of countries at war is not the major source of profit. The desirable volume of income is found in the reconstruction of the country itself, not by national companies, but led by large international construction companies. A large number of them belong to the large monopolistic groups.

The neoliberal religion has grossly modified the traditional principles of the free market. In the global configuration of wealth, the economic South coincides exactly with the geographical South. Africa is the shameful and shameful image that reflects the mirror in which the pretentiously named developed countries are looked at.

Chapter VII. An Afternoon at Taif

"It's a strange purpose to pursue power and lose freedom."

- Sir Francis Bacon. English philosopher and politician-

The boardroom of the oil company Esso -Standard Oil-, located in the imposing Rockefeller Center building in New York, is a large and comfortable space. The general manager, Monroe Rathborne, unilaterally took the decision to lower the price of the barrel of crude oil by **10** cents. of a dollar, agreed for the commercialization of oil all over the world -posted price-. It was 1960 and the big oil companies were in charge of the extraction, refinement and distribution of the product worldwide.

Their position of pressure was oligopolistic, as was the usual practice at the time, with a majority presence of large emerging companies. The arrogance and myopia that characterized the decision would irrevocably mark the future of the western world. A month later, the rest of the big companies, British Petroleum, Shell, Mobil Oil and later Aramco, gathered in Libya, adhered to the decision, signing an identical agreement. Unconsciously, they had opened the way for the birth of the ´*Organization of Exporting Countries of Petroleum*´ -OPEP-.

The Venezuelan Prime Minister, Pablo Perez Alonso, upon learning of the news, expressed verbatim: "rays will fall from the sky". He promptly requested a meeting by the then leader of Saudi Arabia, Abdullah Tariki, to lay the foundations for the founding of OPEC, which took place that same year in Riyadh, the capital of Egypt. Shortly thereafter, the events began to unfold and Tariki himself would be removed from office. In the summer of **1967**, during the six-day war -the Yomki Pur war- the Arab armies suffered a profound humiliation at the hands of the Israeli army. Egypt, Syria, Jordan and Iraq were defeated. One of the most Machiavellian politicians in all history, Henry Kissinger actively intervened in the preparation of the confrontation.

It was a quiet afternoon in Taif. At **1,800** meters above sea level, and 1 hour's drive from Jeddah, Ahmed Zaki Yamani, Saudi Arabia's chief executive, in that year of **1980**, was at home. He was therefore comfortably dressed in a silk tunic and slippers. The silence of the environment seemed to deny that the outside world was experiencing such a convulsive moment. Educated, like most Arab leaders, in the best Western universities, he was perfectly aware of the fact that the more complex a system is, the more dependent it is on the sources of energy that make it work. Never more true, it was exactly the case of the total dependence of the western world on oil.

There were different reasons for this, but the constitutive characteristics of oil, its multi-functionality to be used not only as a fuel, but also in a wide range of industrial processes in diversified sectors, including plastic polymers and textiles, did not explain the phenomenon. There were deeper reasons, such as the conviction of the West, that Arab countries belonged to the third world. Once again, one perceived, breathed in the atmosphere, the contempt and the arrogant and arrogant attitude of the West towards Arabia.

Yamani thus recalled the immediate decision, one week after the defeat of the six-day war, to proceed with the embargo on crude oil, of all those countries that did not support the Arab army. The world oil crisis of **1973** would be the first of many. Nothing would ever be the same. At that meeting, they had grouped around Arabia, the United Arab Emirates, Libya and Kuwait. Algeria and Iran, their direct and traditional enemy, would then be admitted. All together in the face of a common enemy: the West. At that meeting, fundamental issues for global functioning were discussed, such as inflation, the state of the money market, rising unemployment, hunger as the ultimate sign of inequality, energy and natural resources in the process of industrialization.

Algeria showed its most belligerent attitude. It represented for Africa, the same as Vietnam for Asia, but lost. In any case, important meetings had taken place with the aim of reaching agreements between consumer and producer countries during **1977.** The first, in Paris, with President Giscard D'staigne present, and sealed with a resounding failure. The second, with Robert Mc Namara, then president of the World Bank and Willy Brandt, German chancellor, held in Washington. The third was staged in the Persian Gulf itself, with two OPEC leaders present, Sheikh Yamani and his Kuwaiti ally. The result was equally negative.

It could not be otherwise, while the West talked about money, the Arabs talked about religion and values. Western ignorance of Arab culture continues today. A world crisis originated, from which the West has not recovered. However, against its will, the first oil crisis originated by OPEC, in its attempt to influence the world economy and its leaders, had the opposite effects to those intended by the Arab world. The golden age of capitalism- which extends from the end of the Second World War until the beginning of the first energy crisis ended abruptly.

Until then, the traditional economy used global demand as a fundamental equation, which it considered simple variables such as domestic consumption, investment, public expenditure and exports. The two opposing visions of the economy, known until now, the neoliberal and the interventionist, considered identical influential factors in the growth and modulation of the economy. In this way, the USA had overcome the financial crash of the **29´** and later, the exit of the Second World War.

The different governments, had contemplated as a simple equation, obtained, through the modification of simple parameters, the desired effects. The two great enemies of the classical economists were sufficiently well controlled: the unemployment rate and the growth of inflation. But the western economies had never before faced an energy crisis, that is to say, a crisis produced by an uncontrolled increase in costs. They had no theoretical instruments or heuristic or practical tools for solving this new situation, unthinkable until then.

The Keynesian interventionist policies proved to be impotent even for the theoretical approach to the problem. Neither could the neoliberal theses offer answers, but two logical fallacies coincided in their purest style. The first, as usually happens, it was thought that if an alternative is not revealed as valid, then its opposite will be more useful. Secondly, the main thesis of the ideology defended by Hayek was promoted, the reduction to the minimum of the State and the impulse of private initiative, led by companies. In other words, macroeconomics gave way to deregulators measures applicable to microeconomics. In short, this fact, together with the arrival in power of Margareth Thatcher in the United Kingdom and Ronald Reagan in North America, would finally shift the balance in favor of neoliberal principles until the great stock market crisis of **2007**, when Keynes was resurrected.

The intervention of the State was necessary and fundamental for the government of a financial world that was riding out of control.

The theory of complex systems affirms that the contraction of the best implanted system always harms the weakest component. The primacy of manufactured products and the consequent global contraction would relentlessly and permanently damage the third world. A world of which Arabia considered itself an integral part. Jamani's own world. But the process was already irreversible.

Toshiro Doko, president of Japan's Keidanren -Japan's premier institution for instigation and knowledge- declared in **1980** his willingness to engage with the Arab community. The question was obvious: ¿what could the two cultures have in common? The answer was also obvious. Culture, will, sensitivity and awareness of their own history and their weight in the decision for the world's future. The conclusion, the impossibility of connecting in the same development, at the same speed and in an equitable way, an essentially diverse world.

The decision, in essence, consisted in the adoption of pragmatic and local measures for the different peoples. Arabia would negotiate with the Americans an agreement for the rest of the world to pay for crude oil, using the American currency, ´petrodólares´. At that meeting, Arabia requested the technology transfer necessary for the development of the third world, of which it was a part. The transfer never took place and even today, today, it has not taken place and never will. In this way, Arabia would accumulate wealth during the period when its natural reserves were useful. At that time, they accounted for **43 %** of the world's crude oil supply.

For its part, Japan would make a decisive commitment to the development of a society, based on research and development, on an unstoppable path towards the knowledge society. Today, an economy without natural resources ranks third on the world stage, behind North America and China.

Chapter VIII. Blurred Images

"It's not enough just to tell the truth, but it's better to explain the falsehood."

- Aristotle. Greek philosopher-

Japan is an archipelago made up of **6,852** islands, located east of Asia, in the Pacific Ocean. It does not possess natural wealth, however, there has been talk of ´Japan miracle´, which has become the third largest economy in the world, with sustained economic growth of around **8.5 %** a year for many consecutive years. The simplest explanation for such an achievement lies in his conception of work and his deep convictions, which imply the habit of performing individual function, with collective sense. When a Japanese citizen travels anywhere in the world, he does not consider his experience finished, until he tells his experiences with his group of friends and considers their comments.

The island of Aicha in the western part of Japan is one of the most visited in the world. The reason for this is the location of the central automobile factory Toyota in this geographical point. ´Toyota Motor Corporation´ was founded on September 23 of **1933**, in the moment in which ´Toyoda Automatic Loom´, created a new division dedicated to the production of automobiles, under the direction of the son of the founder, Kiichiro Toyoda.

In the business management literature, has become a theoretical confrontation, already classic, the schematic opposition of the productive models ´Toyotism-Fordism´ and above all, the philosophies and principles underlying each of them. The production of the Toyota factory is totally mechanized. Only the intervention of human operators is used for the observation and surveillance of productive robots. On the contrary, ´*Ford Motor Company*´, founded in **1911**, was based on the concept of chain production by human operators. The first studies of times and movements were applied there. The Taylorist methods found a unique breeding ground for their application. The unitary work, reduced and standardized to the maximum, allows the indiscriminate replacement of one operator by another, at any time and any location. A coherent application of the liberal principles of its founder, Henry Ford I.

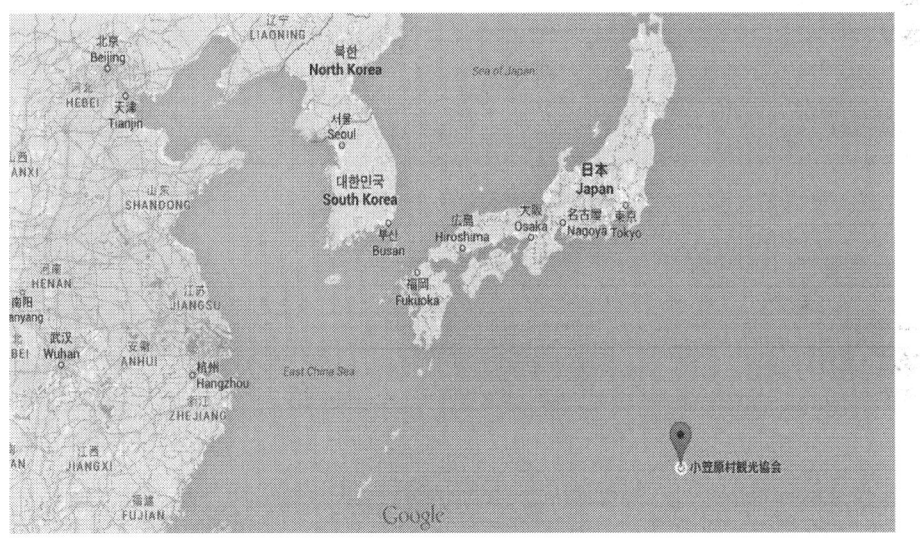

Japan is a nation formed by a multitude of small islands located in the Pacific Ocean. With no natural resources on which to base its economy, it has oriented its growth towards the technological development provided by the knowledge society.

Ford represents, by its own merits, the productive ideal of neoliberalism. Apart from the very presence of its founder, in ideological circles related to the prevailing economic philosophy of the beginning of the century in the United States. Both companies obtain economic surpluses in their activity. The Western mentality is more favorable to the use of human work, regardless of its nature, as the traditionally accepted way to obtain a salary, the basis of individual and family sustenance and consumption.

Likewise, for years, voices have been heard, which are amplified at the present moment, about the danger of excessive industrial robotization, which will inevitably lead to the substitution of man by machine, with the consequent loss of work and jobs, leading to economic disaster. A new example of western myopia.

Toyota with part of its economic profits, has created in its community, a university for the formation of the population. It is not a question, as some reductionist critics state, of training programmers and computer technicians. Society now needs, and will need in the future, professionals and craftsmen such as cabinetmakers, plumbers, bricklayers and workers specialized in the current professions. But it will need them, updated in the latest technologies.

Following the neoliberal logic, the new information and communication technologies -*TIC's*- already generate millions of new jobs all over the world. The central question, then, is not how people are used to obtain a decent wage, but logically, in what quantity and for what purpose, the economic resources obtained from work are used. Logically, there are exceptions to this principle. The main one consists of the perverse and criminal use of child slaves in the production of globalized consumer goods.

The fordist system, faithful to the neoliberal tradition and methodology, made the base of its production rest, in repetitive works, standardized until desperation and giving place to the application of the studies of times and movements to the work of the production chain. In short, it elevated the model of mechanical work, devoid of the slightest degree of motivation that was not economically incentivized. It is true that in later times and up to the present moment, it has undergone progressive changes and not only that, it has gradually incorporated technological advances and the different motivational theories proposed by the behavioral sciences, as well as by the discipline of Business Administration.

Notorious examples are the techniques of 'work enrichment' or previously, the doctrine of 'human relations'. The rectification and adoption of improvements is actually a necessity for private enterprise. In a transnational corporation, survival becomes the basic objective. Unfortunately, this principle, which generates substantial changes, cannot be applied to public organizations, which inevitably drift towards stagnation and departmentalization. They sail towards ports, where remoteness with its constitutive objectives becomes the norm and not the exception.

However, the fact that we wish to highlight is that a conception of work must be adjusted to the very configuration of the ideology of the society in which it is anchored and fits. In this sense, Toyota responds directly to oriental values. The human conception as a set of values, such as respect for ancestors and the wisdom obtained through experience. It is a two-way street. Work represents society, the continent and society as a whole; it is enriched by both economic and social benefits.

A distinctive example, such as dormitories for young workers, who have not yet achieved the possibility of economic independence, would be unthinkable in Western countries. Respect for the group has made it possible for substantial innovations in business conception to take place three decades ago.

Toyota was not only the company that implemented the control of ´0 stocks´ -called *'just in time'* - but also began to contribute to the collective work, the conclusions of individual work groups, the well-known ´Quality circles´ that were subsequently extrapolated to other western factories and it must be pointed out that with a high degree of success. It is convincing once again that the achievement does not have to do with a single isolated manifestation of social activity, in this case, work, but rather obeys, at levels of greater breadth and depth that define the cultural system of a given social group.

This fact has decisive implications for the firm establishment of two of the erroneous arguments, firmly established in contemporary western culture. The first, refers to the use of machines or robots, in the field of work in particular, but in the social sphere in general, diminishes the jobs previously performed by a human being and consequently, harms employment. This prejudice is objectively false.

First of all, robots perform mechanical and repetitive tasks, which people discard because they generate fatigue and alienation. Second, the insertion of a series of robotic stations immediately requires a person or group to control, monitor, program and repair them. It is about the proper and effective use of the human being and the machine for the functions that they can competently perform. The machine repeats indefinitely, the human being watches, supervises and improves.

This belief, as is the case with many other social perceptions, fosters an unusual fear of technological development. History clearly shows opposite conclusions. The list of biological, social and economic improvements, since prehistoric times, does not require much effort for their demonstration. Above all, however, attention must be paid to the fact that the focal point of the production model does not lie in the degree of robotization of the assembly lines, but above all in the use of the economic surplus generated.

The destination and management of production margins or capital gains, are focused in Japan, in addition to the usual government items, to incentivize the ′programs for development and investigation, I+D+i- programs, the unquestionable basis for the future knowledge society.

Chapter IX. Under the Microscope

> "Most often, the limitations we impose on ourselves are the most important ones great obstacles that we have to overcome."
>
> - Aaron Sloman. Jewish philosopher-

The Second World War was a key event in the course of the post-modern era. It was both a drama and a revelation. It is the cause and consequence of the development of human activities and attitudes, as well as of the course of history itself. Until then, the dominant cultural paradigm, the standard of liberal philosophy, was rationality, more specifically, *'instrumental rationality'*, the cornerstone of the axiomatic postulate of continuous progress. Human beings, thanks to their ingenuity and innovative faculties, created technology that led them along a straight path, or towards the utopia of uninterrupted progress, in a time that, far from the classic format of a cyclical scheme, presented itself cleanly linear, in the sense of the march of progress.

Sociology in particular and science in general, based on the paradigm of Newtonian mechanicism and unquestionable individuality, are unable to explain not only the magnitude and significance of the holocaust, but a much more worrying fact, its irrationality. It begins as the logic of Kuhn's scheme affirms, a change of paradigm.

From Germany, the Frankfurt school, supported above all by Frank Horkenheimer, proposes an emotional approach for the explanation of human behavior, as opposed to the classical current, giving rise to critical sociology. He exposes that precisely the detonating mechanism of behavior is not rational, but emotional, that is, irrational.

Psychology had moved in the same direction. Sigmund Freud, in Vienna at the beginning of the twentieth century, had beaten the coherence of rationality, in an inelegant and hardly acceptable way, for the orthodox and orderly environment of the progressive society, universally announcing that such low and degrading impulses as sexual emotions, besides being a subconscious seal, dominated the conduct of the human being. In short, the human being and the animal were only separated by a matter of degree.

As if this were not enough, a colleague of Horkenheimer´s work, of Latin origin, another famous sociologist, Adorno **(1968)** begins to mention a generic variable of personality, the *'authoritarian personality'* as an element of the emotional baggage of the subject, in its most accused point it names 'fascist personality', arriving to measure it by means of a questionnaire denominated scale F -F corresponding to the initial of Fascism-.

In reality, and by definition, personality variables were outside the rational domain. Eysenck, a psychologist of English origin this time, had proposed two of them that are still valid, extroversion and neuroticism. As if that were not enough, the human being not only behaved irrationally and casually, but also in a neurotic way. The picture is completed, thanks to the experimental results coming from the ethology with Conrad Lorenz at the head. In experiments carried out with animals, they showed increased levels of aggressiveness and violent behavior, as a function of the overpopulation index, in reduced territories.

Without being confirmed in humans, it is accepted by extrapolation that in the face of competition for reduced resources, individuals and groups of humans can behave in the same way. In short, it is the recognition of the importance in the underlying behavior and decisions, the influence of the emotional sphere, much more determined by instinctive behavior than the extolled and overvalued, rational faculty.

This conclusion is not at all new and is reproduced in different areas of human behavior. In economics, one speaks of ´rational election´ to justify decisions to buy or to save and invest, but impulsive buying emerges as an unquestionable reality. In political conduct, especially in the *vote behavior´*, the recognition of the emotional vote prevails. Similarly, in social psychology and especially in consumer behavior, an attempt is made, through marketing and advertising communication, to awaken the basic emotions of the consumer and direct them towards over-consumption and, in many cases, to create new offers of products and services, previously non-existent, which are euphemistically called ´acquired needs´.

Reviewing with distance the facts, it appears and not in a surprising way, that the human being, is an evolved animal, concretely a superior mammal. The cold and objective observation, indicates that consequently, we share with the rest of superior beings, a series of characteristics, necessary and possible of the survival. The syndrome of reaction to threats to survival, the habit of aggressive defense of our family and a complex neurochemical system, capable of carrying out actions that are difficult to explain in normal situations. The fact that evolution has turned humankind into the most perfected being, into the most sophisticated machine in the known universe, has actually been possible, thanks to instinctive behavior, to generic behavior shared with the animal kingdom.

We have proposed a simple scheme, differentiated by levels, with the sole objective of allowing us to go a little deeper into social behavior and describe its determinants, in order to enable, at a later moment, a broader understanding of the different situations described here. We have called this simple model MASS -*Simple Systemic Analysis Model*-. It is evident, from our previous book, that we consider that the theory of complex systems, as it is, the world we live in, is the most adequate and possible model for the analysis and description of the present world.

Thus, in the lower part, the instinctive level of behavior is established, which through ´socialization´, or incorporation into social life, through education and training, defines us as suitable members to join a sociocultural system in which the individual participates, in an increasingly active and progressive way.

The process of socialization, then, consists of administering and modulating instinctive actions, which are often presided over by selfish and pleasure-producing behaviors. The observation of children's conduct is revealing, in terms of playful behavior, immediacy in their demands and general motivation, aimed at covering their basic needs. In the same way, they show a wide range of development possibilities, which unfortunately are wasted in a model of constricting socialization of children's potentialities. All in all, the process implies a continuous process of learning the prevailing norms in the ´*society of elderly*´.

The period of adolescence, means a traumatic adaptation, characterized by the difficulty of assuming norms coming from authority figures, among them, the parents of the same gender, that clash strongly, with the feelings of independence, experiential anarchy and desires of self-realization, to the margin of norms and established corsets.

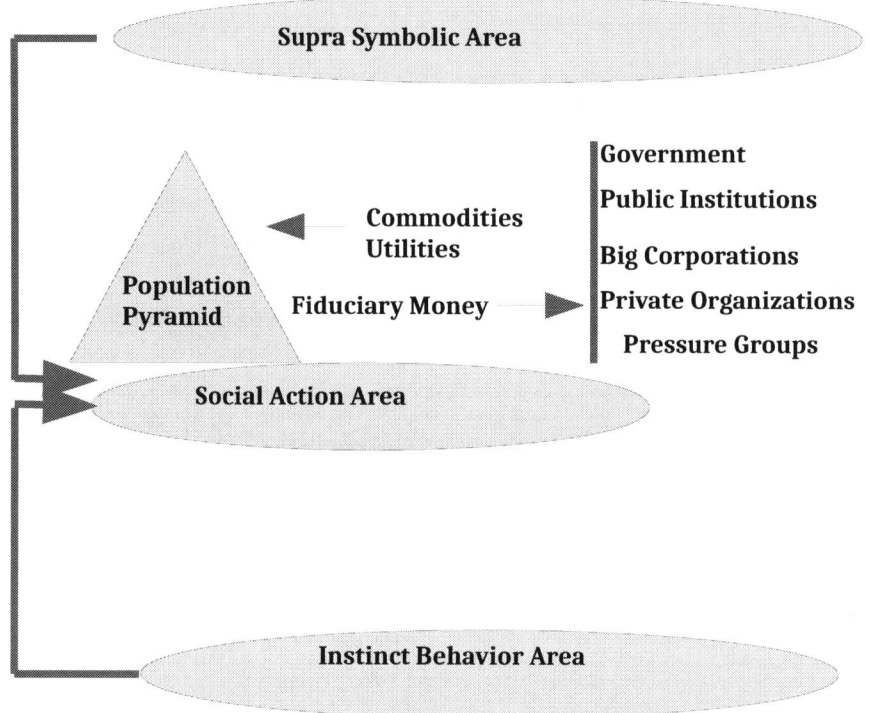

Simple Systemic Analysis Model (MASS) that reflects the three levels involved in social behavior. This is produced by two basic processes. The socialization of the instinctive behavior of young people and the normativization coming from the symbolic sphere that contains the laws and norms that govern the behavior of the different social actors.

The area of social action -the intermediate area in the schema-, focuses on the behavior of individuals and groups. The initial gear of the system is placed in the imperative of covering or satisfying the needs of the social collective. The history of human evolution, is marked by the search for the satisfaction of those needs. One of the first theories of human motivation - *Mass Needs Theory*- has been used for its explanation, since it schematically presents an adequate model of the type of needs of the human being. The social system in subset, must cover the needs of the subjects that compose it.

The first needs, of lower origin and therefore more generic, belong to the instinctive level described above. These are lower order needs, specifically physiological and safety needs. Included in this category are food, clothing, shelter and reject against external aggressions of any kind, climatic, of individuals or asocial groups and any other.

The next group, social needs, begin to be largely uniquely human. The need of ´social relations´, is shared with certain animal species, especially higher order. As primates and lions, homo sapiens, lives in groups, although that if, increasingly larger. As it is ascended in the scale of needs, it is observed that it is required the coexistence in an advanced society, that in function of its degree of development, is self-imposed the duty to satisfy the needs of ´self-stem´ and of its members.

The social system, in order to cover the needs of the individual, requires an endowment of actions, aimed at the transformation of the ´natural resources´ fundamentally aimed at food, the production of other elements such as medicines, the construction of housing for shelter or clothing, for the defense of climatic aggressions.

Likewise, it institutionalizes a series of services, mainly of a health and educational nature. The set of services requires a series of 'channels' or established ways to reach the group of citizens. The latter pays the service provider, generally companies or institutions, through 'fiduciary money', which pays either directly to the provider or via taxes, if the provider belongs to institutional and/or public services.

The set of needs to be covered, however, is relative. Above all, in the needs of type *superior* and to a lesser extent, also in those included in the bottom or physiological needs. The second pyramid included in the graph reflects the social position, normally linked to the socioeconomic class.

Although alternative parameters may be used to define the social pyramid, such as academic training, the most commonly used social criterion is that of social class. Needs vary qualitatively and quantitatively, depending on the position that a given group or individual occupies in the rank of social class. The demands of products and services of the 'highest classes' are greater in number and differentiated in quality, in general more sophisticated.

The products are not only for their utilities or specific functionalities, but fundamentally, for their capacity of representation or symbolic. Thus, a car, regardless of its commercial brand, fulfills the basic function of geographic displacement. But its level of representativeness and social ostentation varies in a recognizable and public way depending on the notoriety, positioning and public image of the commercial brand. In the automotive market, different brands are associated with social status, benefits such as safety or sports lifestyle.

The same phenomenon occurs with a large number of trademarks, organizations, social clubs or membership groups. The economic classes, located in the top positions of the social pyramid, show a greater sensitivity towards the group of needs called ´acquired´, to the extent that the creation of new needs has become one of the usual objectives of commercial marketing and its generic instruments, among which we must highlight commercial information systems and advertising communication. Described in this way, it does not seem to represent a serious problem, beyond the possibility of expenditure measured in monetary availability.

Extended to a global scope, it is a serious flaw in the global system. For example, a western child consumes **400** units of energy more per day than a child living in a sub-Saharan area or country. This fact applies fundamentally to energy of ´vital´ units, that is to say, to food, clothing and complementary products, including hygienic and assistance products in general.

In this way, and as has happened throughout history, the system that initiates, maintains and contributes to the progress of societies and cultures has a marked commercial sense. From this point of view, the barter economy gave way to the mercantilist exchange and later to the market economy. A system drawn, as on this occasion simply and schematically, does not seem to offer any kind of interference or serious problem for its functioning and acceptance.

This impression is a logical perception, since the intervention of human feelings and passions is not introduced into the scheme. the intervention of human feelings and passions. The real complexities, on the contrary, begin to emerge from the first phase of the exchange process. The necessary ´competition´ and producer of improvements, according to the economic principle of the free market scheme, begins adulterating itself, already in the phase of production and supply of services. It does not only obey the law of the stimulation and necessary competition.

Likewise, it happens with the *'commercialization channels'* of the different products and services. The big companies and corporations, normally have, and this norm is applicable to the processes of commercialization, of greater resources and technology than the small producers, in order the production and commercialization of foods, hygienic products, medicines, garments of confection and any other product, being the greater domain, the greater the technological exigency. As can be seen in the daily purchasing behavior, the product offer is led by major brands.

Added to this, distribution companies, such as large supermarkets, put pressure on small producers, in terms of prices and qualities. The general result is the inequality of commercial competition, which leads to the progressive disappearance of the small producer and trader. The guarantee and regulation of the rules and standards of commercial activity and coverage of individual and social needs must be substantiated in the national governments.

Without any kind of doubt, the circumscription of governmental power, to its geographical scope of action, endorsed by the configuration of the nation-state figure, should be without any kind of ambiguity, total. For this reason, the figure of the government enjoys the conjunction of the three types of powers, which cover the normative areas of the performance of the social system as a whole and which are postulated as independent from each other. Legislative, executive and judicial powers.

The application of the set of norms and provisions is channeled to the social set through *'institutions'* and *'corporations'* of a public nature. This normative-institutional set, conforms a figure that does not have real physical substrate, called *'State'*.

The picture is completed, with the presence in the social panorama, of private institutions, whose primary function may have objectives aimed at mediating in the process of conciliation of private and public rights, such as the *'groups of pressure'* -lobbies- or 'unions'. The *'bank entities'*, deal or should deal with the flow of money in both directions of commercial exchange.

Taken as a whole, this seemingly simple framework clearly results in a complex system and it really is. It is therefore subject to the generic laws of complexity. The first of which is the interaction between its components. By way of illustration only, and added to the distortion of unfair competition exercised by large corporations over the rest of commercial competitors, a long series of perversions and adulterations of the theoretical system of social configuration or structure can be added.

The first, to begin in the sense of a more generic spectrum, resides in the transformation or loss of natural identity of the figures that make up the social whole and, therefore, of their primary functions. The *independence of governmental function*, does not take place in its habitual behavior. In a practically institutionalized way, the government, in its executive function, directly influences the two complementary powers. It influences and controls the legislature and, of course, the judiciary. The banking entities become relevant pressure groups, as suppliers of currency and credit, both for the own 'governments' like for the different social agents, among them, the *'politic parties'*.

The *'pressure groups'*, common in all Western countries, and whose original sense, is to influence and direct government decisions in favor of private interests, include not only organizations and specialized service agencies. Their composition is very broad, with diverse signs and interests.

The already denominated *'unions'*, organizations and *'professional colleges'* and *'No Governmental Organizations'* (ONG's), make up this complete epigraph and try to influence the governmental decision-making power.

This functional complication is directly linked to another characteristic feature in the history of social evolution. It illustrates the fact that the goodness or effectiveness of a political or social system does not lie in its formal adequacy but, rather, in the inherent difficulty of concretion or implementation. In that sense, the totality of political ideologies and therefore, social theorists, would show their agreement with the great general statements, frequently used in public discourse, as is the case, of the primary objective of social action, consists in the achievement of the general welfare of the individual.

The difficulty obviously lies in its instrumentation, in its operationalitation, in short, in the way in which its implementation is articulated. A clear example can be seen in the emergence and fall of totalitarian state systems, whose greatest exponent, the Union of Soviet Socialist Republics, has lasted exactly **72** years.

Returning to the proposed scheme, the social system anticipates and condemns, through *'laws'* and *'norms'*, unacceptable or disorderly behavior. The ultimate objective of the legislature is to preserve social normality and to stop any conduct that deviates from the habitual and normalized line of behavior. And this end is applicable to any order of social actuation.

Without extending into this point, which would give rise to a wide debate, the laws, their meaning and promulgation, obey, for the reason of influence mentioned above, to particular and oligopolistic interests, and not to the general principles that sustain that same power, which are materialized in the benefit of the entire social collective. The adulteration of the norms of social dynamics leads directly to corruption and if violations are protected or neglected, to impunity, whether of an administrative or criminal nature.

The set of laws that regulate social action are contained in a series of written documents accepted by social consensus. The third sphere comes into play here, the higher level regulator of social action, which we have called ´symbolic supra-system´. The purpose of ´laws´ is clearly instrumental. Its basic meaning focuses on becoming a tool, an instrument regulating social behavior. On the contrary, however, when a series of prescriptions or norms are institutionalized, through writing and tradition, they undergo a profound transformation, only present in the human mind.

They become artificial constructs, regulatory symbols. They are rarefied, thinned, transmuted into an untouchable principle. This is the case of the document, which represents the law of laws, the national constitution. Again, the cultural substratum of each specific country modulates the way its constitution is treated. Normally, the rule of direct function of democratic development and facility of modification of the national constitution is fulfilled, among other reasons, by the necessity of adaptation, reflection and modulation of the sociocultural changes, that we must remember, are produced to a high rhythm, in exponential growth and not gradually, not in linear evolution.

Once again, our country encounters serious difficulties in internationalize adjustments in a document written at another historical moment, with differentiating perspectives and with totally different motivations, carried out by political representatives, some of them coming from a dictatorial and oppressive stage.

The symbolic level contains other instruments regulating social conduct. One of them has historically conditioned national conduct, fundamentally in the political and economic spheres. We have had the opportunity to observe how the Bretton Woods Treaty has marked the global sociopolitical agenda and continues to do so today. Once again, two proposals for new agreements, generated in the cradle of neocapitalism, the USA, try to condition to a greater extent the globalization of the deregulating principles relating to goods and capital. The TTIP -*Transatlantic Trade and Investment Partnership-*, the Transatlantic Treaty on Trade and Associated Investment and the TPP -*International Transactional Agreement-*.

Ultimately, both seek the creation of specific bodies for the specific arbitration of businesses, of an independent and autonomous nature, thus establishing a bridge to the laws of the entity that at the time represented an appropriate coverage for economic interests: the Nation-State. They represent, essentially, one of the last attempts for total freedom of exchange and economic-commercial expansion, faithfully following neoliberal economic principles.

As a previous and constitutive step of the different existing worldviews, we find the books or ´religious structures´. In essence, they represent a whole set of prescriptions and above all, proscriptions on morals and social conduct. In their different forms, they affect more than **4.5** billion people, two thirds of the world's population.

A more realistic interpretation would mean that the real fact is that it affects the entire world population, since the large group that declares itself an atheist or agnostic, bases its own personal assessment on the rejection of such writings.

Finally, the prevailing worldview contains the way in which each individual or group interprets the reality it observes, including such definitive principles as the meaning of the concept of the other, of that which is different, the weight of the collectivity or social group and the relevance of universal, individual and coexistence values. We have dedicated a previous chapter to the definition and construction of the neoliberal system of thought and the moral style it entails, the utilitarian ethics.

Chapter X. A Formula for Success

> "Man's heart needs to believe in something and believe lies when it doesn't find truths to believe in."
>
> - Mariano José de Larra. Spanish writer-

The different spheres of reality seem to find suitable formulas and geometric forms that represent them, to adapt and respond to the main conditioning factors of each specific level of action. At the macro-physical level, the one corresponding to great realities, such as the universe, dominated by the law of universal gravitation, the sphere, slightly ellipsoidal, like the Earth, is the most physically efficient form. However, in the molecular or micro-physical plane, the carbon structure similar to the cube, resistant and ferrous, has been the basic brick on which the enormous building of organic life has been built.

The social structure, especially in the area of human social relations, there are many forms of organization and government. We recognize, almost automatically, the hierarchical structure, in the form of a pyramid, which is habitual in companies and society itself. In both, the apex is narrow and progressively widens as it descends, until it reaches the base, where the social collective, made up of the entire population, is located. This design also serves for a geographical reality, such as a country, a world scope classified by the economic wealth variable, or a large company.

Large companies, especially transnational corporations, mostly adopt a structure called a network organization, whereby each specific department, regardless of the country in which it is located, depends on its homonym, located in the headquarters or parent organization. In this way, the large corporation combines both types of structure in a given country. The hierarchical organization, in which the general director assumes the responsibility of authority over the entire organization and at the functional or activity level, establishes a network structure through which the central departments or areas control the counterpart departments existing in each country, whether they are production plants, commercial networks or information and administration systems.

The vast majority of multi and transnational corporations have two overlapping structures. The formal structure assumes hierarchical power and all its departments depend on the general direction of the organization. On the other hand, the functional organization depends on the corporate headquarters, thus facilitating its effectiveness and agility in communication, thus avoiding intermediate steps, duplicities and communication errors.

The global financial elite adopts this last organizational model. It is by far the most effective model in terms of coordination, and at the same time the most expensive in terms of resources and energy needed for its efficient operation. Control, through a centralized organization, requires economic, temporary and human resources. On the other hand, cohesion is maintained due to the community of interests, but fundamentally, to the remuneration in economic and social terms of each member of the structure.

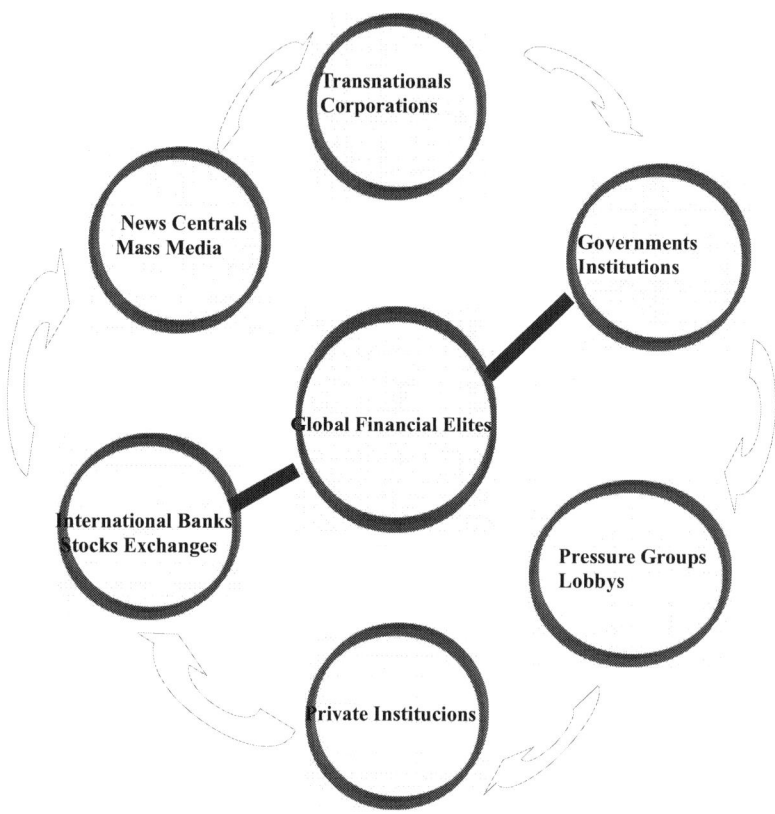

Network structure adopted by the international financial elite. Direct links avoid distortions in communication and demand a high energy cost. The scheme does not exclude intercommunication between the different groups, once the general objectives and strategies have been established, but rather facilitates and promotes them. This characteristic is essential for the effectiveness of the system.

Networks, regardless of their class and magnitude, that is, regardless of their scale, understood as connections between identical nodes or elements, are governed by a common principle. A minority of the elements that make it up group most of the connections. This quasi-genetic rule constitutes a *power law*, known as *Pareto Law* or also, as law of **80/20**. Indeed, in the electrical networks, which supply energy to homes, companies and institutions, the power stations, group the greatest number of connections, necessary for their distribution and addressing.

In human physiology, the brain and, secondly, the eyes, also constitute central nervous synapses or connections, in number greater than **90%** of the total connections. In the case of social networks, the structure of the connections is established by the method of *preferential election*. A minority group of web pages, group the greatest number of visits of Internet users. The prescribers or *influencers* - popular characters -get a number of followers or contacts, coming from the general public. In the case of scientific specialists, a small number of authors accumulate such an overwhelming majority of bibliographical citations that they have originated the study of the so-called *invisible colleges* in a specialty called bibliometrics.

The case of international capitalism intentionally incorporates into its network the institutions and organizations with the greatest power of communication and economic influence over the average citizen. The formation of a structure of the level of complexity exposed requires several added conditions. The first refers to the long time process necessary for its formation.

It can be approached through the typical case of two of the most popularly known initiators of the system. In the primary setting of old Europe, The Family ´Rothschild´, is a European dynasty of German Jewish origin, descended from the first known member, Mayer Amschel Rothschild, who established his banking business in the **1760´s**.

Rothschild bequeathed his fortune to his five sons, who created an influential international family of bankers, in Vienna, London (United Kingdom), Paris (France), Naples (Italy) and Frankfurt (Germany). Baron David René Rothschild currently runs the family business. In **2003**, under his direction, the English and French family companies merged at ´Rothschild Group´, a global financial advisory group. The company is decentralized and has offices in places as diverse as New York, USA, Hong Kong, China, Abu Dhabi, United Arab Emirates, and Moscow, Russia.

On the other side of the Atlantic and approximately **100** years later, John D. Rockefeller builds his fortune by exploiting the oil industry. He founded the ´*Standard Oil Company*´ in **1870**, and soon after, he proceeded to expand and diversify the business, acquiring tankers to transport crude oil and building the first pipelines. In modern terms of business administration, it performs intelligent vertical integration of the oil business. Intuitively, it had proceeded to an upward diversification of its businesses.

At the same time, and around the same time, other business figures emerged, such as the founder of the bank *J.P. Morgan*, J. Pierpont Morgan, railway communications such as Cornelius Vanderbilt and Andrew Carnegie, who in the same year as Rockefeller, constituted *U.S. Stell*, a company dedicated to the steel sector, and through the strategy of rapid growth, the acquisition of various companies, became the second most important fortune in the world.

Thus, at the end of the **19th** century, the germ of la *global financial elite* was constituted in the United States. In this way, the primary condition of the formation of the elite is fulfilled, consisting in the dominion of different *strategic sectors* of the economic functioning of the global market, which began to become planetary and giving rise to the great process of accumulation of wealth. At the beginning, the dominated sectors included international banking, raw materials and fuels for transport and energy.

The second basic premise in the formation of the financial elite refers to the required family tradition. The global elite is much more and radically different from a united group of arch-billionaires. History and tradition are essential conditions for the incorporation of its members. Participation in other strategic sectors, such as technology, the arms industry or mass consumption, is obtained by different means. The exchange of shares, the foundation of joint ventures or the purchase of competing companies are tools commonly used in business marketing for the formation of a diversified group of companies.

The financial consortium begins to function. In the consumer goods sector, for example, the top **10** multinationals produce and distribute the **100** best known brands of products. Globally, the **500** multinational and/or transnational corporations worldwide invoiced **52 %** of the total goods sold in the world. Another of the constitutive features of transnational companies is that in the upper part of their organizations, they are intertwined. In other words, most of the *'management council'*, are formed by identical persons or representatives of identical groups.

The relationship with political organizations, governments, administrations and institutions reveals a fundamental part of world monopoly power. The role that interests the economic elite of governments is directed primarily and above all others, to *'legislative power'*. Specifically, the enactment of laws tailored to and in favor of their activities and interests. The executive power, however, is of inestimable value, since the function that the government lends to the economic elite is twofold. On the one hand, it legislates in favor of the activity and on the other, it represses, controls and restricts social reaction. The distribution of areas of responsibility in this relationship is clear. The financial elite provides the economic funds, while the government establishes the direct relationship with the population.

There are basically two general strategies for the government's relationship with the community. This is a subject that we will deal with extensively in our next issue. The first question refers to the legitimacy of the government versus society. In that sense, regardless of the role of the ballot boxes and elections, in their usual relationship, governments are covered with a mantle of pretended and non-existent technification.

The administrative processes become muddled and filled with requirements and papers; the reading of a simple official bulletin of the state is an achievement of difficult fulfillment. Norms, dispositions, laws, exceptions, oppositions. There is no such technification, it is an apparent and pretended way, an illusory image that is offered to society, in order to justify such an ineffective management. The ´executive power´, must complement with a general attitude, of evasion of responsibilities, with respect to the most powerful -tax amnesties, subsidies and business subsidies or tax exemptions- the legislation in force, thus forming the necessary impunity mantle for the most delirious actions in any field of action.

From the totality of the theories of State action, at this moment, in appearance, the state-centrism theory stands out, because it gives an apparent protagonism to the national executive organ. The pretended sophistication of the government, hidden in reality, a *´consortional democracy´*. Business oligopolies, financial consortiums and pressure groups direct the actions of the State. It should be clarified here that when general statements are made, such as this one, it seems that the cause-effect sequence is clear, simple and immediate. This is not really the case. The institutionalization of political power comes from a strategy of legalized and above all, habitual corruption of public institutions, manifested in multiple ways.

The ´*clientelism*´ as a method of elitist relationship, is based on the use of influences, favoritism, gifts, bites and above all, in the expression of ´*cronyism*´, concretized in social life. Luxury, appearance and social prominence act as powerful springs of economic action. The premises of the theory of presumption, that is, of the value granted by the social mass to who you are and not to what you are, functions as a motivational mechanism of government. In the same way, the ´*instrumental executive focus*´, represents a mechanism, yes, of essential character, in the power transmission belt. In the Spanish case, the origin lies in the world Troika, which executes from Germany the guidelines implemented by the financial power. Our country, along with many others, obey, showing an attitude of submissive schoolchildren. Presenting the final grades of the annual course, for the signature of the parents and approval of the teachers.

If we were to represent the social agenda, that is to say, the list of the problems that any society must face, among them and mainly ours, could be done perfectly, by means of two parameters or continuous, that would be represented by the poles of consensual-impositive style and the proactive-reactive attitude. It is easy to guess where the point of a neoliberal government is located, backed by an absolute parliamentary majority.

Against the fallacy of the affirmation, of the majority in the vote in the democratic elections, it is possible to include in the social dialogue, the relation between legitimacy, effectiveness and governability. Democratic legitimacy is an unquestionable basis of principle.

The assessment of effectiveness corresponds to a large group of collectives that have not exercised their institutional role, albeit for understandable reasons. Opposition political parties and significant social agents, such as trade unions, have also obeyed internal interests and not the reason that justifies their existence, which consists of constant work in search of the general good. The result is institutional inefficiency, which no advanced social system can withstand or afford.

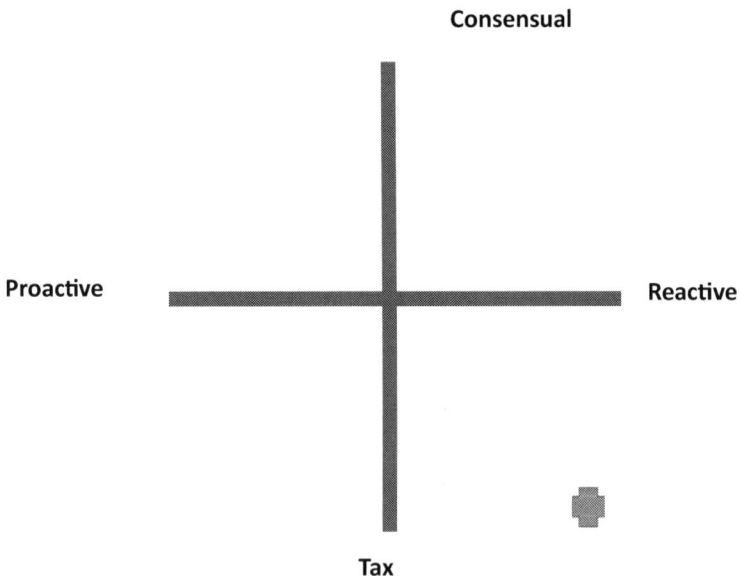

The result of the Social Agenda action of a neoliberal government with an absolute majority, characterized by the government acting through a decree law in the absence of parliamentary consensus and dialogue with representative social agents.

The second major chapter of the relationship between governments and society lies in official information, channeled through massive social communication platforms, *'newspapers'*, *'radio'* and *'television channels'*. The first distinctive characteristic of communication is based on the consideration that political structures have of citizens.

The categorization of the collectivity like *'mass'*, with a low level of understanding and much less of reaction. In this way, the predominant attitude is the concealment or deformation of reality, through the strategies described by numerous specialists, linguists, political scientists and sociologists, one of whom, Noam Chomsky, has defined with enough accuracy, the main ones.

In the first place of the list, due to the moral abomination that supposes, it is found, la *'fear strategy'*. It is used above all, in times and electoral speeches, describing a desolate place, chaotic and absolutely unthinkable, for disastrous and threatening, before any alternative ideological option. Essentially, it can be summarized in the maxim *'we or chaos'*. It is a modified version of the principle, used by Angela Merkel and previously by Margareth Thatcher: "it is the only possible alternative".

Similarly, the fictitious contraption of the creation of a *'common enemy'*, which provokes the unitary response of twinned struggle of the social whole, against the pretended potential invader. For the Americans, communism has played this role, justifying through la *'cold war'* any series of waste, war actions and unjustifiable decisions. For all the historical fascism, communism, together with the Masonic movement, have constituted the flag of the national struggle.

Today, international jihadism plays the role of the enemy to be beaten. It should be pointed out that no violent action finds a justifying argument. Much less if its cost is counted in human lives. But it should be noted that the US secret services and their intelligence agencies have financed and created more than one rebel movement, which, over time, has been accused of being responsible for mass attacks and assassinations, including AL-Qaeda.

Secondly, and perfectly recognizable, is the distraction website, for the implementation of which the presence of one of the strategic sectors of the configuration of the elite power scheme is indispensable. They are the central news and mass media. The strategy consists of diverting the attention of the general public from the relevant social problems, through the tactic of the information flood, that is to say, insignificant and dispersed news. As will be seen below, the barrier and actions aimed at increasing the knowledge of civil society is one of the pillars of the authoritarian and coercive exercise of power.

The moments in which unpopular or delicate decisions have to be taken, of great transcendence for the well-being or the economic future, require and to that extent there are false alternatives, such as the problem *problem creation and solution offer*. For example, the enactment of citizen security laws. In the first place, the interested fact is highlighted, be it urban violence or demonstrations.

The second moment, awaits the social or media commentary and the general demand for solutions and finally, the government emerges as the champion of solutions, through the enactment of a law, exclusively aimed at general oppression, with the basic intentionality, of the exercise of an activity of calm government and without anxiety.

The silent expression *´quiet weapons for silent wars´* is ingenious and appropriate. Another obvious and current case is the use of a ´economic crisis´, with the aim of promoting the dismantling of social rights and public services, through the action of cutting benefits, on the grounds that there is no sufficient budget or no place in the ceiling of expenditure. This argument is very topical in our country.

Directly linked to this point, emerges another complementary strategy of great importance, consisting of gradualismo´. For the promulgation and acceptance of an unpopular measure, such as those mentioned above, of economic cuts in the dismantling of the basic services that cover the inalienable rights of society, partial provisions are used, which are gradually applied, little by little, in consecutive exercises and years. The combination of these strategies has been the key to the generalization of neoliberal ideology.

Thus, radically new socioeconomic conditions, characteristic of the purest neoliberal style, were slowly but continuously imposed during the **1980´s** and **1990´s** all over the globe. Minimum state, privatizations, precariousness, labor flexibility, mass unemployment, wages that no longer ensure decent incomes. So many unbearable changes, which would have provoked a revolution, if they had been implemented all at once.

It is relatively simple to expose the strategies of *'psichopolítics'* or the attempt to direct the social collective, since we have had the sad opportunity to live them directly in our country. One of the most common and also related to the previous ones, consists of the postponement, delay or *'decision delay'*. Specifically to defer or postpone the application of the law or regulation, potential solution to a relevant problem.

The first condition consists of the presentation of the future norm as *'painful and necessary'*, thus seeking public acceptance, at the time of communication, with the basic aim of less social resistance in its future application. In this way, the justification is served: "we already predicted". The psychological and emotional motivations, which are used by means of this strategy, are evident. It seems easier to accept a future effort than an immediate demand. In addition to this, there is a widespread tendency in the community to think that the situation can change and improve in the future.

In fact, all the strategies have a common characteristic. The use of *'emotional plane'* more than the rational, in the audience and directly linked to it, to address the public in a childish and puerile tone, seeking reactions of the same level, that is, pursuing the suggestion of the public. The use of the emotional register opens the door to the human subconscious plane, to implant or graft ideas, desires, fears and fears, compulsions, or induce acts.

In the next step and very familiar to our country, is the strategy to provoke or reinforce ´self-blamed´. In the midst of the world stock market crisis, we have had the opportunity to listen to an enlightened member of the technocracy, to use the sentence par excellence of accusing the very victim of the situation, consisting of the fact that the crisis originated because the "Spaniards had lived beyond their means".

We wish to understand in this ruling that many citizens should have rejected mortgage loans, offered by the entire banking system of our country, financing more than the total real estate value, with the sole purpose of maximum and offensive, economic profit by the banking sector, the same that, after the indecent real estate bubble built, has been rescued through the public purse. Once again the application of the neoliberal gold maxim: ´socialization of losses, privatization of earnings´. Again and as a strategic practice, the victims themselves are blamed.

Finally, a strategy emerges, not applicable only to psychopolitics, but to the ideology inherent to neoliberalism and, in reality, to all government movements of ´fascist character´, regardless of their political sign. It reveals itself as an authentic obsession, as well as pragmatic necessity and condition ´sine qua non´, ignorance and mediocrity. In the words of Chomsky "The quality of education given to the lower social classes must be as poor and mediocre as possible, so that the distance of ignorance that plans between the lower classes and the higher social classes, is and remains impossible for the lower classes to reach".

This tactic implies another implicit strategy, as it is, the general stimulation of the social collective, to be complacent with mediocrity, as much relative to their own lives, as and above all, of the political class, which should not be forgotten, is financed with public funds, that is to say, the citizen through his taxes, pays the salary of the political class. An extension of this reasoning leads directly to the bold but unaccepted conclusion, to the same degree as real, that authentic power resides in society, a principle that should not have been manipulated at any time.

The second fundamental characteristic of communication refers to tactics in the use and endogenous characteristics of language. The evocative power of language does not work when the sentences are of such a wide degree of generality that they become sentences of empty meaning. Thus, the messages do not have concretion, they use an indefinite, normative, desirable language, without descending to concretion and much less announcing courses of action and concrete formulas. The following figure is a clear example.

Step 1	Step 2	Step 3	Step 4
Dear companions	the realization of the premises of the program	it forces us to a thorough analysis	of the existing financial and administrative conditions
on the other hand and given the current conditions	the complexity of the leaders' studies	plays an essential role in the organization	of the development directives for the future
Likewise	the constant increase in quantity and extension of our activity	demands precision and determination	of the general participation system
However, we must not forget that	the current structure of the organization	helps in the preparation and realization	of the attitudes of members towards their inescapable duties
Similarly	the new activity model of the organization	guarantees the participation of an important group in the training	of the new proposals
the practice of everyday life proves that	the continuous development of different forms of activity	fulfills important duties in the organization	of educational directions in the sense of progress
It is not essential to argue the weight and significance of these problems since	our information and propaganda activity	facilitates the creation	of the training system for cadres that correspond to the needs
rich and diverse experiences show that	the reinforcement and development of structures	hinders the appreciation of importance	of the conditions of the appropriate actions
the desire for organization but above all	the consultation with the many militants	offers an interesting verification test	of the development model
the superior ideological principles condition that	the beginning of the general action for the formation of attitudes	involves the process of restructuring and modernization	of the forms of action
we might even dare to suggest that	a specific relaunch of all the actors involved	allows in any case to explain the fundamental reasons	of the basic premises adopted
It is obvious to point out that	overcoming outdated experiences	it will mean an authentic and effective starting point	of a whole spectrum of broad spectrum
but we would be insincere if we ignored	an indiscriminate application of the confluent factors	allows in any case to explain the fundamental reasons	of the generating elements

Political discourse is based on statements of the highest level of abstraction and generality, lacking the power to evoke specific contents. It can be verified, beginning with the choice of a certain phrase from the first column, followed by any other present in the second, then the third and then the fourth and a second time to begin and so on without practical time limit.

Eduardo Galeano, expresses with his usual lucidity, the use of euphemisms in the discourse of the elites to the masses "a new torture has appeared with the name of illegal constraints, treason is called realism, opportunism is called pragmatism, imperialism is called globalization and the victims, developing countries and pure capitalism, market economy". Vital and profound, as always.

The evocative power of images that language possesses, since the appearance of symbolic thought in human beings, allows, in conditions of high uncertainty, the appropriation of this characteristic by institutions and the political class. Suggestions of new realities are produced and designed, with pretensions of permanence and verisimilitude in the collective ideology, through the use of new labels or maximalist and frightening terms. The common enemy, communism, international terrorism, crises, the disappearance of pensions; in short, ´*chaos*´.

A falsehood or lie, constantly repeated, not only makes it possible to make decisions that are interested in and harmful to the majority and of broad significance, such as social cuts, the austerity that condemns the countries of the south or the promulgation of a disastrous labor reform, but also and above all else, makes it possible to present reality as a great stage of apparent order, a false screen that hides, as an enormous backdrop for a theatrical stage, a profound *disorder* and social opposition.

Chapter XI. Stepping on the Accelerator

> "We will not be granted external freedom except to the exact extent to which we have known, at any given time, to develop our internal freedom."
>
> - Mahatma Gandhi. Hindu politician and thinker-

The history of human evolution could only be described by following the incessant progression of pre-technology and current technology. Technological progress exemplifies one of the basic characteristics of complex dynamic systems: their exponential growth. This means, in plain language, that growth does not follow a linear development. An apparently isolated discovery produces, through its interaction with the rest of the knowledge, a rapid growth, a multiplier effect and not only an additive one. This is the case with the Internet. The history of human evolution presents four major revolutions that radically affect the perception of the world around us. The first is located in the Middle Ages, and comes from the religious doctrine, specifically Christianity collected in the New Testament.

The space-time dimensions were modified, even before the discovery of Christopher Columbus, who collapsed, the general belief at the time, referring to the flat shape of the Earth. In the Jude-Christian conception, on the one hand he added a fourth to the three primary physical dimensions. Specifically, a metaphysical dimension, such as the existence of the sacred or cursed place- depending on the convenience -but outside the objective reality, called heaven or hell, an adaptation from other cultures, as in the case of the Viking Walhala. With respect to time specifically, the cycle of life was restarted, only for people of faith, the faithful, who would have access to the promised reincarnation.

The second great revolution was carried out by macro-physics -the physics of large bodies- with the theory of Universal Gravitation by Isaac Newton, in the **17th** century. Albert Einstein's theory of General Relativity, already in the **20th** century, was in charge of broadening and deepening reality, providing a premise, which will become germinal, in all subsequent science, consisting of the conviction that any scientific knowledge is always relative. It basically depends on the characteristics of the observation and also -and fundamentally- on the characteristics of the observer.

A frontal shock to this evident reality and even today, surprising was contributed by the micro physics or ´quantum physics´. The physics that studies the particles and the molecular level.

In full year of **1900**, Max Planck, contributed a differential behavior of the particles of light. Later Werner Heisenberg and Erwin Schrödinger, in **1926**, modified in a single equation, the behavior at subatomic scale. It is worth noting that the characteristics that govern this physical level are in complete disregard of the laws prevailing in the macro world. Strictly speaking, the dimension of time varies, from the moment in which a particle, can and in fact occupies the same position, that it already occupied in a previous moment. But above all, the rule that governs this plane of reality is indetermination, that is, the objective event can be any, within a range of probabilities of occurrence.

Thus, if it were transferred to the plane of human experience, an event would have the same probability of occurrence as its opposite. Hence, the well-known paradox of ´Schrödinger´s Cat´, consisting in that due to the probability of indefinition, if a cat were locked in a closed box, it would not be known if it would be alive or dead, until the very moment of opening the box. From that moment on, the objective of theoretical physicists has been to look for a theory that unifies all the existing forces in the universe. The theory of everything, was Einstein's obsession until the moment of his death, and gives title to a recent film about Stephen Hawking. We hope at some point in another installment, to be able to talk about string theory, which seems to make this attempt, but for that, you need to handle a minimum of 11 spatial dimensions and at least **2** temporal. So much for a relaxed reading.

The following revolutions that affect the structure of reality and consequently, in modifying at least some of the parameters of the known world and also impact directly, on the beliefs strongly implanted in the vision, above all, western, comes from technology. A qualitative leap in the form of relationship and communications, indisputably, constitutes the Internet.

The first connection between the computers, located at Stanford universities and the Californian UCLA, took place in **1969**. That same year, other partial networks, developed for private and especially military and defense use, such as Arapanet, joined the project.

In **1971**, Ray Tomlinson sent the first e-mail in the history of mankind. Twenty years later, Tim Berners Lee creates the world's first Web site. Nine years later, the Internet has one million users and by **2012**, it is close to **2.5** million. The reaction of large companies has been directed towards the control and use of this phenomenon, obviously for commercial purposes, to the point, which has been called *'informational capitalism'*. And not by chance, but for different reasons. One of the main ones is that only **10** years ago, only one technology company -Microsoft- was among the five corporations with the highest share price. It was accompanied by an energy firm -Exon- and a large international banking group -Citi-.

Today, the five largest companies on the international stock exchange are working on technological development and have grown from its widespread use. While Microsoft maintains its third place, Apple, Google, Amazon and Facebook -familiarly known as the GAFA Club- have joined.

The dimensions of time and space have been radically modified once again. One lives in a society in which mediatism and spatiality have ceased to exist. The offshoring of the economy has been accentuated. It is possible today, in real time, to carry out financial operations in the main stock exchanges of the world. Curiously, the stock exchanges of New York, Paris, London and Tokyo are immediately accessible, to the point that it would cost in terms of time, plus the real presence of the user, even if they were all together, located in our city of habitual residence.

Manuel Castells has correctly defined this feature of social globalization, as the *'network society'*. The near remoteness, is an accurate euphemism, to categorize a new social structure, which at this moment, is difficult to value its cost, in emotional and psychological terms.

The use of the net has meant an authentic hatching, a detonation of barriers and rules that regulated practically the totality of the fields of human action. Social analysis, which implies a value judgment, is not easy.

The emerging fact is the freedom of information and action, at the same time, that a greater control of our behavior and intimacy, on the part of the technological giants and its real consequent, in a mercantilized world like the present one, of the commercialization and sale of the personal data, to all that company that pays the demanded monetary cost.

In strictly political terms, one of the worst devils in the neoliberal imaginary of the elites has found a form of realization. An informed society, historically, has been the worst enemy for any ruling elite. A society formed and informed, presents attitudes and consequent actions, significantly uncomfortable for the formal power. The judgment, the opposition, the justified and coherent alternative, the demonstration in the media and on the streets, crystallize into significant obstacles to institutional power.

The various spheres of power have tried to adapt quickly. From ´Deep Internet´, illegal trade and computer piracy have been revealed as constant activities. They lead the dark reverse of the phenomenon, a feature common to almost all technology. With great probability, the ambivalence in the technological advance, has in the use of the atomic energy, its most flagrant case. In short, its control and regulation is difficult. Governments, institutions of all kinds and large companies are subject to constant cyberattacks.

But innovations coming from technology, affect conceptual nuclei, which until now, formed immovable pillars of traditional beliefs. In February **2001**, the ´*human genome project*´-PGH- published the results to date: a **90 %** complete sequence of the **3** billion base pairs, components of the human genome.

The PGH Consortium published its data in the February 15, 2001, issue of the journal *Nature* The project had its ideological origins in the **mid-1980´s**, but its intellectual roots go back much further in time. Alfred Sturtevant created the first genetic map -an authentic genetic cartography- of the mosquito ´Drosophila´.

Undoubtedly, the decisive step in the molecular analysis of the genome consisted in the discovery of the double helix structure of the DNA molecule -*Deoxyribonucleic Acid*- carried out by two authentic idols of scientific research, Francis Crick and James Watson in **1953**. They deservedly received the Nobel Prize a little later, in **1962**, in the category ´physiology or medicine´, shared with another researcher, Maurice Wilkins. We had to wait until the 70's´ to be able to sequence DNA, an objective achieved by Frederick Sanger, who awarded him his second Nobel Prize in **1980**, this time in the specialty of chemistry.

The ´*genetic engineering*´ or biotechnology, represents an angular and determining scientific specialty, for the present life and its future, both in the medium and long term. Medicine is one of the disciplines that has contributed to a greater number of applications, such as, for example, the generalization of the use of ´insulin´ in **1982**.

Genetic engineering currently has a very broad spectrum of applications, including perhaps the most notorious, consisting of the cloning of complex organisms, such as animals. It is also used in the cultivation of food and in the treatment of basic ecosystems, soil and water, allowing hitherto unknown advances in food production, pharmaceuticals, animal and plant breeding and the development of biofuels.

Artificial intelligence probably represents an ancestral human tendency, the production of organisms similar to man. The initiator of the investigation in this matter, was the British mathematician and cryptographer Alan Turing. During the Second World War, the German army had developed a method of encrypting messages, based on the machine called ´enigma´.

The German military superiority forced the Allied high command to try to decipher the complex encryption. On this occasion, it brought together a group of experts made up mainly of linguists, mathematicians and computer scientists. While the rest of the team approached the solution to the problem by means of decoding and text interpretation techniques, Turing focused on building a machine capable of interpreting the meaning of the messages by means of algorithms, i.e. complex sets of rules.

Certainly, chance helped him in an unsuspected way and with few words present at the beginning of all the messages, he managed to decipher the rest. The number of lives saved by allied combatants was enormous. In 1950, once the war was over, he published his experiences in an article titled ´Computational Machinery and Intelligence´.

Alan Turing, died prematurely, due to the prejudices of the time with respect to his condition of homosexual and directly, of the medication that he was forced to take. His work was continued, already in the United States by John Von Neumann, during that same decade. The line followed in his main contribution to the area of research, constitutes in reality, the beginning of a tradition, still not completely abandoned today.

It consists in the construction of ′*programmables machines*′, whose physical base, organization and functioning, tries to imitate the structure and functionalities of the human brain. The anthropomorphic trend. Thus he designed the first computer programs that a computer could store in its memory.

The merit of diverting the attention from research to the capacity to process information by itself corresponds to the neurophysiologist Warren Mc Culloch and the mathematician Warren Pitts, who laid the foundations for the design of the first neural networks. At the Darmouth congress, organized in **1956** by themselves, the basic assumptions of the specialty were established.

For the first time on the planet, it was publicly recognized that a highly complex phenomenon such as thought could occur outside its fundamental structure, the brain. Consequently, in a machine. The implications of this statement, especially for traditional religions, will be dealt with independently. Secondly, it was recognized that the logical and thought process can be understood and therefore explained in a rational, scientific and logical way.

Those derived from these assumptions are several and complex. In the first place, if thought becomes synonymous with learning. In the **1980′s**, one of the first complex machines, ′*Logic Theorist Machine*′ demonstrated a capacity for innovation, with respect to its initial guidelines, provided by its basic programs, solving some of the rational problems proposed by two of the best-known specialists in formal logic in history, Bertrand Rusell and his companion and friend, Whithead. According to the specialists, the first mechanical apprenticeship in human civilization had taken place.

In the study of artificial intelligence, one of the most pronounced tendencies in human beings stands out, affecting very diverse areas and phenomena of study. It refers to the tendency of facts and objects to *'anthropomorphize'*. It constitutes a natural inclination to attribute and interpret similarly to human qualities, observations and features of objects or symbols. Religious iconography is a clear example. Statues can be *'pious or cruel'*, the sea can be *'raging'* or the destination can be *'fair'*.

Specifically, in the field of artificial intelligence, we speak of *'sensors'*, *'logical processes'* or *'learning'*. There are no such traits. Only the machine responds to original programming algorithms, by means of responses that have previously been indicated to it that they may be acceptable, by logics. Thus, computer programs have been designed, capable of playing checkers and chess and, of course, of providing strategies applicable to armed warfare. Cinema has made brilliant reproductions of some of these skills. The consequences of personalization of facts, entelechies and conceptual constructs have far-reaching implications. Some of them directly affect one of the greatest and oldest human longings: the *'achievement of immortality'*. Sufficient time and space will be devoted to this issue, hopefully in the near future.

The dream of human procreation was completed with the appearance of the first mobile robot in **1962**, called *'Shakley'*. The obvious difference between a computer and an articulated robot is that the latter must necessarily interact with objects in a three-dimensional physical space. But not only this. In an attempt to reproduce the human way of acquiring knowledge, la´manipulation´ of objects has opened a path to generate cybernetic knowledge.

The essential question lies in the fact that a machine is only a set of *'physics circuits'*. Unlike the human being, in which the biochemical system is decisive.

Even accepting the principle of fashion among programmers and developers, that 'all' what you can imagine, you can *'program'*, the structural complexity and also conceptual, of the programs required to simulate a complex behavior of intelligent machines, requires a lot of storage space. 'nanotecnología'ha has come to the aid of robotics and artificial intelligence, enabling a large capacity for storing information in increasingly reduced spaces -*chips*-.

The attractiveness of the potential for development of AI -artificial intelligence- has such depth and implications that since the **mid-1970's**, it has become an area of interdisciplinary study. Philosophers, mathematicians, logicians, linguists, mechanics and, of course, programmers, have been passionate about its study and development.

The combination of several scientific specialties, nanotechnology -study of microscopic systems- physics of conductors and materials, artificial intelligence itself and robotics, have achieved high level achievements in the present. The wizard of an intelligent telephone seems to understand the questions we ask and is capable of generating answers, which seem appropriate in an endless sequence. But it is convenient to establish a first general nuance, in the drawing of possible panoramas of application of the set of these specialties of study. The applications are invaluable in tasks that require accuracy and incessant repetition. The applications of industrial robotics are a clear example.

Nanotechnology has followed a similar trend of development, the microscope and its own evolution, allowed already in 1936, to observe reality, with degrees of resolution close to the dimensions of the atom. In this progression, technicians from the Massachusetts Institute of Technology (MIT) began to use the term of ´molecular engineering ´. Texas Instruments, built in **1958** the first integrated circuit and its industrial use, has been since that moment, constant.

Farther, more powerful, smaller, to the point where Feynmann -a prestigious theoretical physicist- speaks of the manipulation of objects ´atom to atom´. The atomic computer, or better quantum, is already a reality. The term nanotechnology, coined by Norio Taniguchi, of the Tokyo Scientific University in **1974**, opens an almost endless threshold of surprising applications. Crystals in the immediate future will not require cleaning since their nanocomponents will repel dust.

Applications for health and medicine are also difficult to imagine. Surgical operations, with the implantation of sensors at the molecular level, are already being carried out. Likewise, the University of New York is working on the construction of the production line, as if it were a production factory, DNA chains. Cinema and science fiction in general have endless material here to imagine. Making a simple projection, the combination of these technologies, represents in large part the fulfillment of the ancestral dream of the human being, directly directed to prolong his life, in both senses, in quality and length.

Throughout modern history, technology has been the object of in-depth study. One of the most outstanding conclusions, consists of the highest directive rule of innovation, denominated *technological imperative*, which basically expresses the fact that everything that can be done, will be done and everything that can be done will be done. The second significant question refers to the well-known principle of *technological neutrality* which expresses the erroneous assumption that technology is in itself neutral and depends on its use and the objective pursued with it, the results obtained.

Not by chance, there are dramatic examples of the falsehood of that assumption. Perhaps the best known, already mentioned above, is the use of the discovery of nuclear physics, which allowed its criminal use in the Second World War, with the use of the atomic bomb, bombing the cities of Hiroshima and Nagasaki. Its effects, on the descendants of the murdered population, persist today and the real scope and persistence of the genetic malformations they originated is unknown.

The review of the achievements obtained by the technological advance as a whole, practically forces the imagination, the projection of possibilities, sometimes disproportionate. So much so that different initiatives have already taken place, reflected in meetings of multimillionaires from all over the world, with the aim of achieving what we call 'the dream of alchemist'. Overcoming the physical threshold of death. Eternal life. In fact, more than one well-known scientist has stated categorically that "the first human being to live more than a thousand years has already been born".

The theoretical design of the project seems clear and simple. It would consist of transferring the experiences and memory of the subject to a cybernetic organism -cyborg- and living in a virtual way. Virtual reality has become evident as an option for leisure, distraction and work, of considerable value. On the other hand, the media and, of course, the entertainment industries, mainly the audiovisual and written media, have found in this option an inexhaustible vein.

A well-known means of communication, highlighted the emergence of the *affective programming*, since a robot, was able to respond to the different moods of its owner. Here, two common practices in human communication and perception are combined. The use of generic labels and generalized scientific misinformation. In this case, in fact, the objective and concrete fact is that a complicated programming algorithm, indicates to the robot, a correct action according to the position of the 45 muscles that compose the human face and that are used, to reflect an emotion in an instinctive way. The computer only interprets the millions of combinatorial probabilities. A complex but unintentional fact.

In any case, the question would be: ¿can an emotion be programmed? The answer is drastically, no. It is perfectly possible to program simulations of all kinds, which require the analysis of huge amounts of data. Currently, the commercial actions and also social and political, use the ´massive analysis´ in real time of big data, for decision making and implementation of very important rules and actions. Likewise, the achievements obtained by recent technologies reach unsuspected levels, unthinkable only **20** years ago.

Brain surgery has managed to implant a nanoreceptor in a patient's brain, which makes programmed vision possible. They have also been applied to a wide range of injuries and dysfunctions, both motor, perceptual and affective.

Simultaneous translation is now possible through small instruments. Intelligent cars, which perceive objects and communicate with each other, have advanced prototypes. Special mention should be made of three-dimensional -3D- printers, capable of constructing not only buildings but also complete production factories and, above all, human organs, suitable for transplant, using genetic material, which does not produce any rejection in the receiving organism, precisely due to their individualized origin.

The increase in the life expectancy of the population will continue to increase in a linear manner. Cell regeneration and the use of stem cells has obtained results practically similar or close to the total reversal of cell deterioration and aging. The improvements obtained in transgenic foods have made a particular contribution. Aging is produced by cellular oxidation. If cells regenerate or new cells are born, the aging process could at least theoretically be reversed, if not maintained. Likewise, pharmacology progresses continuously, through more advanced and novel chemical compounds.

Biomedicine is on the right path to achieve another of the old human desires: the constant search for happiness. The level of quality of life in people with affections and illnesses and of middle or advanced age, has become literally prodigious results.

Developments in the applied sciences and especially in those areas that require a basic or indispensable technological contribution, are costly in terms of economic and temporal resources.

The process of launching a new pharmacological product has a cost, with the logical variations depending on its objective, around 8 years and 5,000 million euros. But the economic benefits also reach an astronomical level. Actually, the fictional future of clinics, which provide joint treatments for the mind and body, including virtual reality, are not so far apart in time. But in the present, the big technological and pharmaceutical companies fight for what could be properly labeled, like the "eternal youth". It is not a pill, but a set of conditions of life.

Once again, if that ideal state is materialized in a reality, it will only be available to a few billionaires. While this fact occurs, unfortunately, it seems that the technologies best used by the extractive elite are geopolitics and global engineering, that the detested pollution, cancer, traffic accidents and of course, that the over-population, measured in terms of death and life suffering.

Chapter XII. Myths and Legends

> "Do you want to be rich? Well, do not be anxious to increase your assets, but to decrease your greed"
>
> - Epicurus of Samos. Greek philosopher-

Money as an exchange unit, as well as a unit of value, constitutes one of the greatest agreements that humanity has achieved in its long evolution up to the present time. Its use, was generalized by the Phoenicians, due to its great commercial activity and its growing expansion, about the year **1200** a. C.

As with much of human activity, it requires broad agreement for widespread use. Motivated in the first place, by the comfort, the necessary confidence in its validity, has been extending throughout the history.

Its role as a unit of measurement has produced a curious change of functions. In reality, and for that same reason, money or representative currency, constitutes a means to an end, which consists of the good that you want to acquire. But because of the breadth of existing goods, it has transfigured its meaning into an end in itself. Money is normally used in the so-called real economy, that is, in transactions between people and companies, but due to its function as a good in itself, it is listed on the stock exchange.

Traditional economic theorists, as well as governments and international organizations, have tried and of course succeeded in transmitting the idea of economic crisis, as specific and cyclical situations, own and congenitally associated with the characteristics of the economic system itself.

The possibilities of manipulation of this idea, as widespread as it is false, are considerable for the established power. They are used as a political instrument, for a large number of purposes, among them and mainly, tax increases and the absence of socially necessary actions, such as public investment in social policies. Nothing further from reality. There are no such crises, as derived, punctual and less cyclical elements.

They constitute a structural weakness, always consistent with the abuse and perversion of the foundations of the general economic system. The governments establish a simple agreement with the different National Central Banks.

The government grants the function of issuing currency, usually paper money, and as a counterpart, the central bank finances the government's economic needs, such as, for example, the payment of the payrolls of public employees. Once the officers collect their respective salaries, they enter their amount in different private banks. The private bank, following its normal commercial activity, must lend money to generate business. In this way, it grants loans to its clients for the acquisition of goods or other necessary expenses, such as materials for general or university study, acquisition of assets or assets of the company and others.

In the case of the private client, one of the most common purposes is the mortgage loan, that is, for the acquisition of a home. This is so, for various reasons, especially due to a cultural factor, in which property has become a distinctive class sign. It is true that in some countries, unlike most of Europe, land prices are even among the modalities of rent and purchase.

At the same time that the bank grants a loan to a client, the first irregular and distinctive situation to highlight occurs. Money has, at that moment, 'two owners at the same time. The depositor and the applicant of the credit or borrower. Thus, the only way for the bank to return the money, if the legitimate owner requires it, is for the mortgage borrower to enter the quotas established in the commercial contract on a regular basis. For this reason, in times of economic recession, banks adopt a non-concession policy, despite the fact that the interest rate established in this case by the European Central Bank is, at this time, negative. A case never seen in economic history. That is to say, that the private bank is a creditor of the European Central Bank, in case of requesting a loan.

The amount of money that the private bank can lend, is regulated by the 'cash ratio' established by the monetary authorities - central bank, national securities commission. At this time, it is at **10 %**. This means that if a client enters a payroll of 1000 euros, the bank by law, can lend 900 euros and must reserve 100 euros, to provide the different circumstances in which liquidity is required, such as cash provisions, made by customers, either through cashier's checks or credit cards at ATM's.

Another precision is necessary at this point. The most common way in which the bank carries out its operations, consists of mere electronic transfers, in simple accounting notes to any other bank, in which the social agent, individual or company, has an open account. In the previous example of the mortgage, the concessionaire of the mortgage credit electronically transfers the amount of its price to the bank with which the owner of the home operates.

Periodically, the credit sector and in particular, the banking sector, performs a total balance operation, or regularization among all of them, in which the debtors pay the deficit to those banks with surplus, while the entities that have balance 0, nor they pay or they do not charge. This operation is identical to the one performed in the international balance of payments, called *'clearing'* -claimed-.

In order to approach the magnitude and overall volume of money in circulation, it is convenient to keep in mind the number of companies of all types and sizes, which pay their payroll by the same procedure - required by recent law- and the number of private banks existing This at national level as international.

Thus, if each financial institution -banking or not- that follows the policy of granting **90 %** of the amounts deposited by its clients, to other clients as a loan -since in reality, the bank is a supplier or marketer of money, that is to say, that money is its product- it can be understood that the total number of operations and the resulting total economic volume reach levels that are difficult to quantify, both nationally and globally.

Mortgage loans are linked to the purchase of land, one of the values that hardly lose market value. On the contrary, its commercial qualification rises continuously, which is why, together with other equally scarce materials, such as precious metals, it constitutes, under normal circumstances, a safe investment. In economic terms, it meets one of the basic requirements of appreciation of the traditional economy: its scarcity. In this way, a large bank in need of liquidity can issue public debt, for an amount that contains all the remains, of the deposits it has as a cash ratio or for all the mortgages granted. A large private bank or an Investment Fund can acquire a considerable number of mortgage debt and enter it into the financial markets, that is, launch it for exchange listing.

The stock exchange or market is, in essence, a magical world, since it can produce, like any other company, innumerable products, with the difference that it is quoted for an estimated value, not for a real object. The bank or fund that has acquired the mortgage debts, can create another product, associating the original with a mortgage basis, another value, such as an investment fund for retirement. At that time, a *'financial derivative'* has been created from scratch.

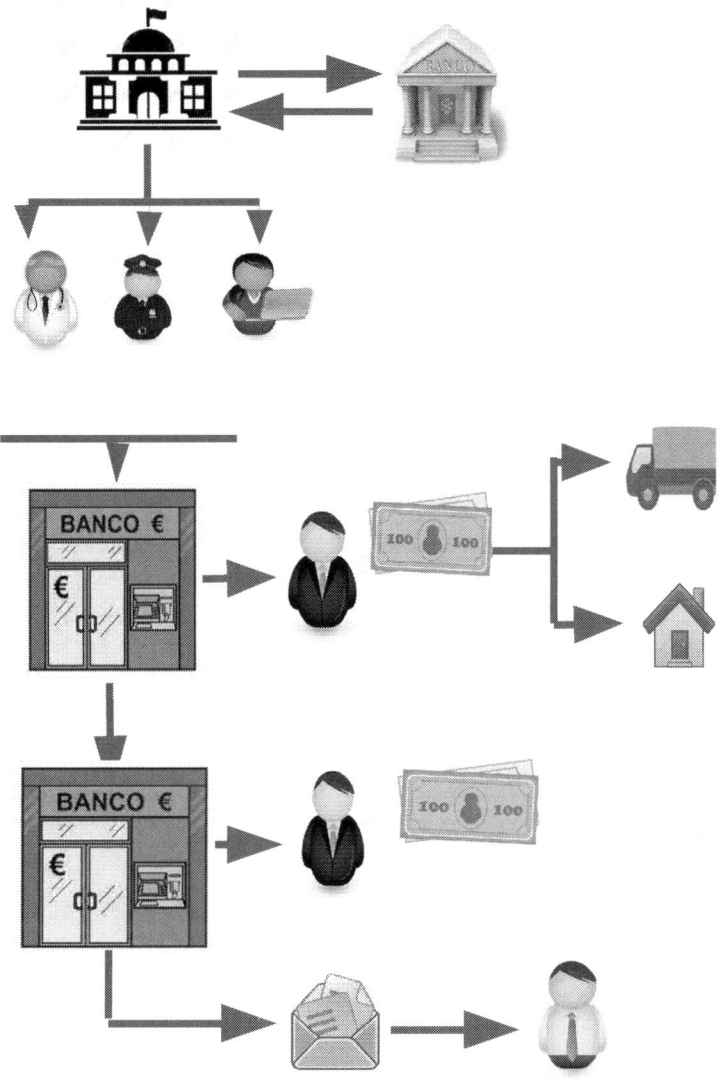

Flow of money circulation. Private banking is only required to maintain a low cash ratio or reserve guarantee, therefore, it lends to another debtor the remaining amount, which at that time, already has two legal owners. A large bank or investment fund acquires a large number of safe securities, mortgages guaranteed by the good land, always stable or upwards and offers its quotation on the stock market, either alone or linked to another value such as a retirement fund. From the increase of loans to potentially delinquent debtors, the circuit of falling stock values begins.

The chain of new existing stock products is very large, but the only indicator that determines its expected result rests on the nominal value of the shares. The purchase-sale game is determined, depending on the convenience of the investors.

Until then, everything works according to the inherent dynamics of the bag itself. The imbalance begins at the moment in which a certain bank or number of banks, with the sole objective of increasing their profits, begins to grant mortgage loans to clients with doubtful return capacity and at the end of the trend, to clearly delinquent clients. At this moment, the subprime mortgages are born-a suitable translation could be *'secondary or derivative mortgages'*.

Even in this case, the new product is cataloged by the 'international rating agencies' such as Moodys or Standard and Poors, according to their estimated security. In this way and as indicated in the figure, financial products that incorporate only mortgages or a simple combination, such as mortgages plus investment funds, would be classified as triple A, triple B or triple C, depending on the estimated security of collection. Even in this case, there are Risk Funds, specialized in acquiring risk products, since as in any type of bets, the rule of *'greater risk, greater potential benefit'*, in other words, the more secure securities, applies, by accumulating more capital and having a higher price, pay lower dividends to investors and shareholders.

The New York Stock Exchange carried out one of the magical operations that allows financial perversion, originating the beginning of the biggest financial crisis since the crash of 29. It designed a financial product called 'CDO' -*'obligations collaterized by debt'*-, consisting of in three groups of mortgages, of different levels of risk, that act as a waterfall. First fill the quota of the first, then the second with the surplus of the first group, and finally, if there is enough quotation, the third group.

The artificial illusion continued, through the creation of more derivative products, consisting in the division of the original products, dividing them in half and recombining them, so that the new products mixed the different types of risk, becoming invaluable as a whole. Despite the continuous warnings of the possible consequences of risk, Raghuram Rajan, the first broker who issued a repeated warning, the indiscriminate proliferation continued its path, for clear reasons, although it may be that with the perspective of time, they are incomprehensible.

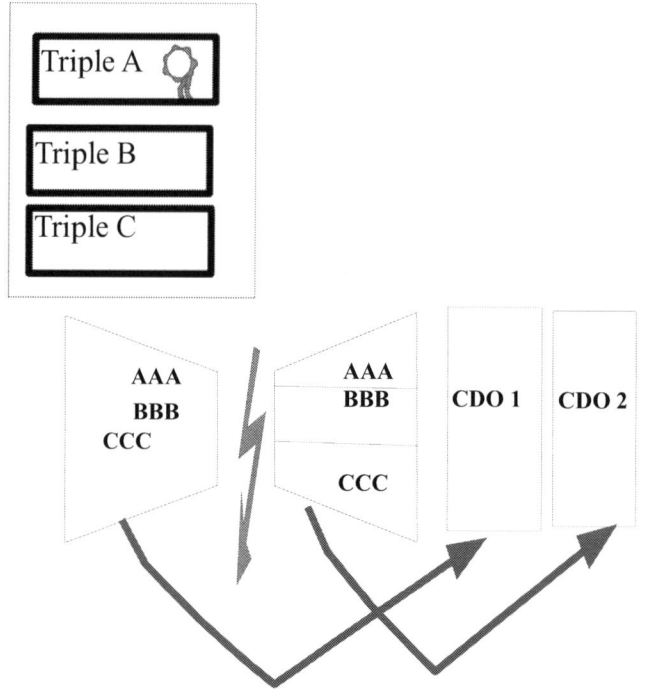

The magic of Wall Street is nothing more than a consummate perversion of the financial market, in the great circus of illusion represented by the stock market. A package of stocks or bonds classified vertically, with different types of collateral or risk, is divided into two parts and re-combined so that the differentiated classifications are lost and diffused throughout the derivative product, multiplying this same action indefinitely.

The stock exchange, has a quote as a whole. Similar to the GDP of a country, the more activity it registers, the higher its total index, expressed in a quantitative score, so that the way of maintaining the different national ratios of the stock market, -Ibex 35, Nasdaq, Nikkei, Dow Jones- consists of maintaining a high level of activity. Thus, all the paying securities obtain gains proportional to the values acquired.

At the beginning of the last great world crisis, the great American banks and financial groups, were perfectly aware of the potential chaos, each time of greater dimensions, but with the double objective of maintaining the stock market index and obtaining profits in the case, of If the situation were maintained, they began to acquire this type of obligation. Those entities holding shares also knew that the only existing mechanism, to maintain the nominal value and avoid general panic, consisted in not releasing the bonds for sale. In other words, the strategy to maintain a fictitious equilibrium lies in not initiating a movement to sell obligations and in this way assure its permanent value.

The well-known names of Goldman Sachs, Lehman Brothers, J.P. Morgan, Deustche Bank and especially some regional banks acquired obligations, aware of the inherent risk. At the moment of trying to get rid of the investment, the worst of the possible fears for a fictitious system, began to expand: distrust.

The banks did not accept the offer from the other banks. The crisis spread to the American currency, in all international markets. Other collateral factors, such as the rise in the price of oil, contributed to the final disaster. The direct consequence, the lack of liquidity in the world system, first of a financial nature, later economic. The recession of credits, became the dominant rule and widespread practice.

The economic contraction, originated his habitual and well-known familiar situations, closing of companies, scandalous losses of positions of work and new *'stantagninflatión'*. The economy stagnated with a rise in prices, motivated among other causes, for fear of the generalized closure of companies. This is the worst possible economic scenario, since fiscal and monetary policies and their application do not obtain the usual results. The next level is still considered as more serious. The 'deflationary' configuration in the face of the loss of intensity of world demand. The most feared scenario for the theorists of traditional economics. The resounding failure of monetarist policy; the actual situation.

In the configuration of the widespread financial crisis, the US Federal Reserve had to start the 'rescue' of the big banks. A new chapter of the repetitive and nauseating practice of neoliberal capitalism; the socialization of losses, in this case, the use of public funds to finance private and fraudulent interests, criminally guilty.

The banking structure had to be rescued with federal resources. An image that perfectly reflects the morals of the directors of the big international banks appeared on the front page of some newspapers of international circulation. Only a day later, after the government announced the bank bailout, the world press published that a senior manager of one of the big banks, a necessary collaborator, in the biggest world crisis of the modern era, had organized a party to celebrate the governmental decision of the rescue of his entity, in a well-known hotel in Monticello, for the whole directive, with a cover price of **150,000** dollars.

At the call of attention of the rest of his fellow managers, finally, he canceled the reservation. But the most revealing result is that once the situation was evaluated and controlled by the government and the federal economic authorities, only one person was imprisoned. He was a second-line manager of one of the big participating banks.

It remains to add another strategy, applicable in reality, not only to the area of financial business, but to the generic commercial field. It refers to the well-known 'pyramidal structure'. A business, regardless of its commercial activity, collects funds from a group of associates. Start a campaign to increase capital, on two principles that work inexorably: the high percentage of benefits and the speed of collection. In this way, while new associates are incorporated, the first group is rewarded with the money collected from the second group, and so on. Obviously, this business works during the time that new partners can be recruited. Normally, it does not last long, but the amount of money defrauded is incredibly voluminous.

Once unsuccessful, the tactic to avoid criminal liability is to protect the legal personality of the company and in the best case, proceed to change the fiscal name and start another business of identical characteristics. And the wheel of fortune, keeps turning.

The biggest fraud in the history of the stock market, using this practice, was led by Bernard L. Madoff who managed to defraud, for more than **20** years, **65,000** million dollars, investors large and small. He was arrested by the FBI in 2008, because he confessed his scam.

The main direct cause of the great world crisis, has been in another perversion of the financial system. The coherence of the current economic system, despite its intrinsic flaws, as we shall see later, must be maintained for its effective, though imperfect functioning. Private or public investments should be destined to the productive sectors and, especially, to those strategic sectors, directly linked to innovation and development.

This tendency has been recommended on numerous occasions and by different specialists. It constitutes the new economic configuration of the already present and dominant in the immediate future. The *'clean and renewable energies'*, the 'research and development', the 'sustainable growth', are some of the alternatives, which evidently clash with neoliberal ideology and practice.

We have addressed the performance of the big banks, focusing on their stock activity only. The issuance of financial products to the general public, not necessarily a great investor, is also a common practice. A wide variety of investment products are available to the small saver. Pension plans, insurance of all kinds, savings plans, investment plans, obligations, public debt, treasury bills, bonds and many others. A great supermarket of money.

Fraud and deception, also in this market segment, has paid territory. The average citizen shows a clear and understandable aversion to decisions and information, referring to money, investment and the economy in general. The veneration and trust placed in the specialists of the economic area is similar to that which health professionals deserve, especially doctors. They idolize and are cause for admiration.

This trust and fervor, has served countless times, to encourage deception and fraud, especially and as a rule, no less indecent and amoral, by repeated, segments with higher degree of ignorance and older age. This has been the case, of the disgusting practice of the issuance of preferential obligations in our country, by a conglomerate of old savings banks, which as if it were not enough, has required a public ransom, which like any ransom, pays the citizens. In other words, the victim of the theft is forced to finance the thief.

At the moment of considering the necessary reform of the Spanish constitution, it should necessarily be reviewed, those types of crimes, directed against sensitive, weak or unprotected groups. The elderly, with little or no training, but with the discipline, responsibility and inexhaustible work to build a country, as is the case of our elders, should be, at least, protected by law. Similarly, the depraved and immoral, to a greater extent if they are organized or belong to social, banking or political institutions, should be subject to criminal sanctions, not only administrative, and all this, with a necessary exemplary character.

Chapter XIII. Obligated Visit Places

> "Instinct dictates duty and intelligence gives pretexts to avoid it."
>
> Marcel Proust. French writer-

Governments, like large corporations, especially in periods of crisis, observe other systems and other corporations, with the aim of copying or at least adapting the essential mechanism that produces isolated success. This has happened in the past years, and states and communities have appeared, with a national operation, close to the model standard. This is the case of the Scandinavian countries. It is curious that suddenly social democracy has been discovered, when the welfare state has been an objective and in principle a utopia, by which the general society and from a historical perspective, has fought in all fields, social, political and even using armed struggle.

The essential questions arise around a central theme in the neoliberal mentality. ¿Can a social system, dominated by a business mentality, in which individuality prevails, achieve an equitable social system, with some similarities with collectivism?.

Again, the answer is affirmative. Scandinavian Peninsula is made up of five countries -Norway, Sweden, Denmark, Finland and Iceland- which are not only a current example of efficiency, wealth and equality, but have represented a historical example. In addition to this, their rates of conflict and crime, are the lowest in the European set.

It should be noted that Norway and Sweden are not part of the European monetary union. They have their own currency. The group of these countries, with their **25** million inhabitants, have managed to design and finance a social system, where social, health and educational services are among their main achievements, in parallel or perhaps because of the obsession they pursue. tail countries in social achievements: a high level of innovation and competitiveness. The powerful institutional development, based on a virtually zero level of corruption, and financed with a high tax rate, is returned to the community, with an indisputable and high degree of protection to the family, subsidies for housing and the fight against social marginality.

The apparent mystery, is not such in reality. There is a strong 'social value', based on equality or better, *social equity*, achieved through consensus among 'social agents', mainly, institutions, employers 'associations and workers' representatives, who have based their agreements on collective agreements, with the option of arbitration. Collective bargaining represents a benefit for the community. It is assumed in a total way by all the social agents and the population, the logical principle that "the lowest degree of unemployment, the highest government income". For this, motivated and satisfied workers are required, to the same extent as responsible and prepared citizens.

Curiously, and as a paradox, the high tax levels supported by the middle class, makes them interested in the performance of the government and in politics in general, in order to supervise the actions and dispositions undertaken, by the institutional set. In this way, the Scandinavian peninsula, has managed to cross the troubled ocean caused by the crisis, in a safe and oriented, without affecting in the least, the fundamental rights of citizens; without cuts, fatalistic alerts or apocalyptic hyperbole. According to the ideal of Eastern life. The Scandinavian society shows a high degree of balance between generalized collectivism and an outstanding degree of individual freedom.

In a new social key, a rule that we understand, which is basic for social engineering and design, is established both in work and in social activity in general. It is the Greek principle of proportionality. The distance between remuneration levels and citizen power is frankly reduced. As we will have occasion to check in a future delivery, the computer simulation confirms this rule. Social stability, it seems even insured, for proportionality rates of **20 to 1**. That is, the difference between the worker with the lowest salary and the highest level of salary must be less than a proportion of **20** magnitudes of value.

Based on values of understanding and social equity, the Scandinavian countries as a whole, although with the logical inter-country differences, have managed to enter into the economic dynamics of the virtuous circle. The *'dignified work'* is the main producer of wealth and this is reverted into training and more work for citizenship. This apparently simple model can not be explained solely by institutional suitability or work coherence. How could it be otherwise, its primary and general rooting rests on the main pillar of the prevailing culture. Adaptation to the time of crisis has been based on the solid basis of a strong equitable culture, that is, collectivist.

Values such as solidarity, have managed to lose the mantle of charitable acts, isolated and caused by the need, to transmute into a solid permanent predisposition, that is, in an attitude. And this in subjects, with a sense of independence and individual freedom, strongly rooted. The image of the modern Viking can be highly representative and curious.

Logically, the accused individuality, in a society in which young people are motivated and subsidized, to achieve their independence from the family at an early age. As a direct consequence, this fact has weakened the patriarchal society, carrying its inherent benefits. The importance of women and their labor development, as much as vital, has reached preponderant degrees. The aids to women with children constitute a strong nucleus of independence and social solidity.

Equality of opportunity, is not threatened by prejudice of class or sex. Organizations of recognized prestige such as UNICEF or Save the Children, report levels of exposure to child poverty, less than **2 %** of the population. Norway has become the best country in the world for motherhood, despite the fact that **47 %** of the workforce is made up of women. Equal parental leave has decisively influenced this situation.

In these moments, in which our country, is immersed in the debate and oriented in the 'Educational form', should consider, with depth and interest, the Finnish education system. The best educational system in the world, according to the dreaded PISA report, prepared by the OECD. The Finnish educational system is absolutely free, in all its stages, from primary education to the university doctorate. This includes dining expenses and transportation.

The key to the success of the education system, falls on the figure of the teacher, prestigious and respected, one of the most requested in the workplace. A 6-year university career and compulsory knowledge of pedagogy have made the teacher an indispensable element of social success.

Equally, the Spanish labor reform, simplistic and erroneous drawing of the economic reality, should have studied the Scandinavian model, generically called *'reflexisecurity'*, in which, maintaining the option of freedom in dismissal and hiring, the company is always protected from labor expenses, but in return, the state is responsible for meeting the needs of the unemployed, under the principle of providing sufficient training, for a rapid reincorporation into the labor market.

In the exclusively economic field, there are qualitative differences compared to the rest of the developed western world. Faced with the worrying data worldwide, which indicates that **1 %** of the population, has **50 %** of total wealth, according to data for the year **2015.** For example, in the US, and **12 %** of the population, holds **84 %** of wealth, while in Sweden, **60%** of citizens with lower income level, possess **47%** of the country's wealth. The causes of the social success of the Scandinavians have been attributed to different generic factors and, above all, to their possible combination.

The first, derived from the Protestant ethic, which emphasizes primarily, individual responsibility, as a primary value. The long democratic tradition, based on the alternation of government, with the Christian Democratic parties, nevertheless shares the firm conviction of state intervention in public life.

Likewise, the society participates actively, in the political dynamics of the country, by different methods, including the popular referendum, which, among other decisions, ruled, a negative sound when entering the country in the European Union.

In any case, it seems improbable an immediate surgical transfer or direct extrapolation of the Scandinavian model to any other country in the world. In Spain, an attempt was made to implement a decade ago, as it had been recommended by the European Union itself. The result was a real failure. The different national societies present absolutely different and specific cultural configurations. The difference in the percentage of GDP, destined to education by Nordic countries and the rest, is, if not abysmal, if really significant, as shown by the data of the World Bank itself. The distances remain, in terms of investment in research and development, which in the ideal situation, are financed by both private and public initiative. In short, different worlds, different results.

Faced with the social democratic orientation, represented by the Scandinavian countries, based on a high price of the welfare state, different alternative strategies are observed, given the monopolistic and monolithic impact of global capitalism. The first, and main defender of neo-capitalist performance and principles, is represented mainly by the United States of America and the European Community.

Secondly, the alternative of the sub-systemic grouping, formed by the BRIC countries, with Brazil, in the process of leading a new South American movement, overcoming the failure of the Bolivarian movement, although at this moment, with its economy in a state of recession. The third representative case, is polarized, by the strategic movement of the countries of the Arab Emirates, led by Abu Dhabi, Dubai and Qatar.

Becoming the top of the range of leisure, investment and business society, the new land of opportunities, surpassing the US, are the three strategies chosen, for each of them. Finally, there would be the PIGS countries - Portugal, Ireland, Greece and Spain- which should seriously consider abandoning the armored and iron corset of the euro, dominated by the Germany-France axis.

The United Arab Emirates, supported by the enormous capital obtained from its oil wealth, have designed a strategic plan for the region that they are applying with great success. Dubai has made a strong commitment to diversification, directed towards an economy based more on knowledge and service, thus ensuring its position, as an important tourist, financial and business center, as well as real estate agent.

The policy of open doors to investment and immigration has turned the Emirates into the new land of promise, surpassing the old American myth. Dubai has become the center of holiday luxury, with a constant activity building luxury sites. Abu Dhabi, has been oriented towards research in new technologies, renewable energy, knowledge society and support of ideas and private initiatives that come from any country in the world.

A small center of business activity, in the middle of the Californian desert, Silicon Valley, has been a point of reference, for decades, for the world economy. The most innovative technological companies have had their birth and development at that point. Maintaining a commendable independence of work, diversified financing and strategic autonomy, they have managed to combine results with total autonomy, in terms of work standards and social environment. Certainly, the image reflects lights and shadows. The great technological giants, continue although with remarkable variations, the path of the global economy, of neoliberal cut.

Finally, China, along with the so-called *'Asian Tigers'*, a group of four countries formed by South Korea, Hong Kong, Singapore and Taiwan, have led economic growth and levels of industrial activity, without historical comparison. There is no shortage of conspiracy theories, which advocate the anonymous protection of the USA, in order to illustrate to the world, about the benefits of capitalism in comparison with the reality of centralized authority. But certainly, they have crystallized in an economic alternative to consider.

Chapter XIV. Reviewing the Script

"let think the people who govern and let themselves govern"

- William Penn. Religious British-

The previous chapters have described the ideology underlying the messages of the financial elite, as well as the delegation in governments, of the direct relationship with the people -that noun unfortunately has lost the endearing connotation it previously possessed-. We have attended, to the different communication strategies used by the administration and the linguistic games and conceptual fallacies, unfortunately manipulated. The characteristics of the sender and the usual political messages have been described.

From the perspective of communication theory, we are required to make a brief annotation regarding the two remaining factors that make up the basic scheme of communication, such as, and above all, the perceptive characteristics of the receiver, the individual, group and segment of communicative interest and also, and no less important, the features of the communication channels used. In strictly technical terms, the physical support of the communication, together with the constitutive features of the communication, constitutes the total message and is decisive in measuring its effectiveness.

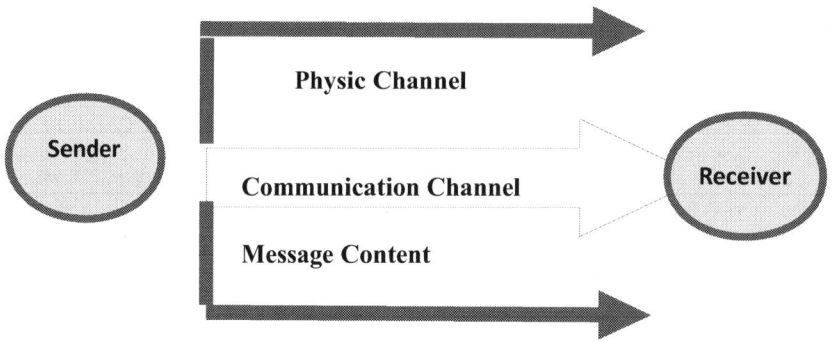

Illustration of the communicative process in the theory of information. A certain sender emits a message, which together with the characteristics of the mass communication channel, television or newspaper, is perceived by a set of receivers. The interpretation of the message is processed according to the characteristics of the receiver, such as desires, attitudes, cultural level and many others. By definition in this same theory, the human being is classified as a highly defective and unreliable receiver in terms of the accuracy of reproducing and interpreting objective messages.

It remains to add, however, two constitutive characteristics of the mass messages. The first one, resides in its sense, which is unidirectional, that is, there is no possibility on the part of the receiver, of immediate response. That does not rule out, logically and by virtue of the content and meaning of the message, there are no deferred responses such as demonstrations or criticisms in other media, or even if the message occurs in certain contexts, such as political rallies, the response is immediate. In addition to this, the relationship between sender and receiver is asymmetric.

The body that issues the content of the message is endowed with formal authority, while the receiver, except for isolated occasions, in which it targets very well-defined segments of the public, is by definition undifferentiated, unarmed, amorphous, from the point of view of the communicator.

Another relevant element of the message and its effectiveness refers to the constituent characteristics of the communication channel used. In that sense, the channels are differentiated according to their specific features. Television, for example, in terms of the symbiosis between image and language, is considered by experts as an authoritarian medium.

The newspaper or magazine is not so immediate, although it may be current. It is not so tax, it can be closed and postponed reading. They are already known, the necessary technical resources, such as declamation and gestural or body language, that political leaders, train with 'coaches' or professors of interpretation and declamation.

Regarding the contents of the messages, a whole team of professional writers, either journalists or screenwriters, make, sometimes, without material time, the speeches of the political leaders. However, natural qualities are required in the leader for communication. Historically, in ancient history, Pericles and Demosthenes, are considered examples difficult to overcome.

In recent history, Abraham Lincoln, Winston Churchill and Mahatma Gandhi, are authentic referents, worthy of professional study. In world history, John F. Kennedy has shown an ability to oratory and conviction, hardly equal.

Together these qualities, to a physical aspect, that transmitted sincerity and credibility. Another American example is the neoliberal Ronald Reagan and above all of them, without discussion Martin Luther King - his speech with the beginning "I have a dream", has become practically a motto and I sing to social resistance. In our country, without a doubt, this position is occupied by Felipe González Márquez, former Spanish president **(1982-1990)**.

At present, and since the beginning of the century, social networks have acquired, for the mentioned reasons of immediacy, degree of generalization, possibility of individual participation and rapidity of their effects, in an essential channel in communication policy, both institutional as private. Governments, political parties and pressure groups, regardless of their nature or corporate purposes, have developed teams specializing in social networks, usually led by the figure of a *'community manager'*.

The fourth and last element of the process, the receiver, represents a beautiful contradiction. The *'homo sapiens'*, evolved from the higher primates, differs in a single gene of the chimpanzee, being this a reality that dislikes remembering and above all, recognizing a large number of social collectives. Share with them, a wide repertoire of responses, markedly animal or instinctive.

So much so, that a series of behaviors referred to priority areas of life, and their respective decisions, are taken mainly emotionally or emotionally, such as playful purchase or impulse, personal and loving relationships, devout behavior, adherence to groups or parties, and a long list of personal decisions, of significant importance.

The relationship with the other and their presence, the need to elaborate complex strategies, in order to hunt and defend their tribe and territory, facilitated and accelerated the acquisition of language, which would progressively configure abstract thinking, allowing the generalization of facts and decisions and developing symbolic thinking. Mental images, from the observation of stimuli and physical and real events.

The symbolic thought, has become a powerful tool of ambivalent character, in a double-edged sword, in a coin of two faces, clearly opposed. In its positive aspect, the own evolution and technical and social progress, are direct result of the capacity of invention, abstraction and innovation, supported in an insatiable need to discover, to know, to investigate and to explore. We have mentioned an almost exhaustive relationship in our previous delivery, of historical achievements in the areas of technology, thought and social, in a general perspective.

The negative aspect of these qualities is the possibility of being handled and manipulated, alluding to their emotions and evoked symbols, by leaders with emotional traits, fallacious arguments and above all, accustomed to being legislated, dominated and subdued by political power and above all, by physical coercion. These traits are well known by the powers that be. In fact, the most successful speeches have become classics, appealing to the threat of a common external enemy, which facilitates the unity of a certain society or fear of an undesirable future.

The perverse management of symbols has constituted a historical trap. The neoliberal ideology has systematically and abusively used the triad 'God, Homeland and Home' as a motivating standard for the great battles, accompanied by other complementary symbols, equally striking and motivating, such as the flag itself, the feeling of national body, the historical personality, the role of chosen by history or any other constructed mental device, and used as a communicative tool and evader of individual responsibilities.

The slogan "God and History will judge me" has been used by well-known fascist leaders, as a justification for genocide, deprivation of freedom and wrongful national development or crimes against culture, property and human rights. Similarly, the facilitation or definition and of course of an imagined enemy, although real, has been a liberator and hyperbolic justifies of wild and unjustifiable actions.

The USA, through the fallacious argument of the *'cold war'*, have justified the arms increase and the invasions and armed attacks, to areas and regions that had nothing to do with ideological rivalry or geopolitical convenience. In any case, there are questions in this sense without answering, for example, ¿whose enemy is Africa? The new enemy, since one is always required, has set itself in the strategic sights, in international terrorism. An enemy created with economic collaboration, military advice and the use of armed forces against legitimate regimes or arbitrarily defined as enemies, or almost always, barely favorable to US economic interests.

In summary, the fact that the human cognitive function, endowed with the rendering of abstract representation of reality, by means of symbols and ideas, that is, of mental models, classifying them into general categories, has been highlighted dramatic example of ambivalent conflict from any perspective from which it is analyzed.

In a recent television debate, an economic expert, innocently assured, that the economic system was not finished, that it was constantly renewed.

Nothing is further from reality. Savage capitalism has its objectives fixed and its methods solved and these are simple, atavistic, ancestral. The dominion by the force and the manipulation of the instincts of the mass society. All this, taken to extremes that challenge all capacity for acceptance.

Social networks have been the object of study as a support for advertising and above all, propaganda understood in the literal sense, that is, as the distorted communication of positions or ideological or political positions. Combined with the exacerbation of compulsive use, they have become a strong antidepressant with massive effects, and maximized in their effects. The possibility of expressing personal opinions in a public way, although without a direct audience, helps to reduce feelings of injustice and perceived pressure. This fact is functionally valid for a significant majority of society.

The conceptual scheme of complex systems theory, proposed in the chapter, fundamentally highlights two facts, which should be taken into account, since they represent, coherently, the keys to the possible modification of the imbalances of the level of social action, that is, of the real facts. The socialization of the individual, is produced essentially by the educational process, in which the training, stands as a key component in its final effectiveness. The process of socialization, is composed of a double slope. As we have already explained, a fundamental part consists of modeling and tempering the demands of instinctive behavior, the rules applied to social behavior, which is also public.

The second and most important, is the formation of the individual, future social being, through education, not so much in rules, but in values. These must be explicit and obvious, but they can be assumed or introjected, through academic training. Traditional education relies mainly on the memorization and learning of disciplinary content and not so much on the conceptual understanding and practice of the knowledge acquired.

Following a principle attributed to Confucius "I hear and forget, I see and remember, I do and I learn". Here, part of the fundamental core of the question is centered. The educational process must have as ultimate goals, facilitate an individual, adaptive and full existence and, on the other hand, the full development of individual capacities. In fact, one of the most widely used definitions of the individual's welfare state rests precisely on the possibility of developing their abilities and aptitudes.

We attend with perplexity, to political discussions, concerning the convenience of education in the secondary phase, about the learning of two or three languages. The third language, like any other disciplinary learning, is learned more easily than the second. Identical reasoning serves for the fourth and fifth. The learning of languages, not only enables communication, with people belonging to other countries, a sufficiently important element in itself. It allows an approach to other values, ways of perceiving and interpreting reality and ultimately, different cultures. It enables, indirectly but substantively, different modes of approach, analysis and problem solving. Educate for life Probably it was Balzac, who ruled that "ignorance is the mother of all ills". The concept is applicable in this case yes, in the opposite sense. Knowledge is the basis of wisdom and what is more important, know-how-the Anglo-Saxon know-how.

In the second place, and in the opposite direction, the regulatory and legislative elements, located in the superior plane of the behavior that we had defined as 'symbolic supremacy', deal with the normativization of the behavior of agents or social actors. Here, rests the second key of immediate community action.

Reinforcing the adjustment of current legislation to social realities, changing and evolving at great speed, appears as an imperative necessity. In recent statements by the Spanish justice minister, he claimed that the penal code, drafted at the end of the last century, was appropriate for the little thief.

The crimes have evolved, as we have had the opportunity to observe, in form and complexity, also in its spectrum of influence that generates considerable damages for various groups, especially sensitive ones. New forms of behavior appear, previously nonexistent or hardly visible, which need to be regulated. *Cybercrimes*, the wrong denomination of gender violence, financial crimes and, above all, unacceptable and unjustified institutional coercion.

In this last line, should be reviewed inexcusably, those coercive behaviors, arising or arising from the institutional authority and above all, governmental, unacceptable and immoral, but above all, unjustifiable in their admission by the rest of social forces. Among them and in our country, they are likely to list a large number of these realities, unfortunately.

The death of **30,000** people, sick of C Hepatitis, for not having been medicated with a specific preparation, Sobaldi, for purely economic reasons. Equally, the existence of **2,700,000** households without any type of income, most of them due to the situation, necessarily result in children suffering from poverty, that is, hunger during the day and cold at night.

The manipulation with lucrative aims of more than 300,000 people, the majority belonging to the third age, by means of the preferred obligations, on the part of financial organizations, rescued with public money, with purely lucrative aims and by means of the intentional deception.

On a second level, although not less important, the numerous cases of bribery, influence peddling, misappropriation of public funds, falsification of public documents, prevarication and a long list of legal figures, all of which involve official or administrative positions, It must not be forgotten, they are posts of service to citizens and subsidized with money from the same social group, which they steal with impudence and impunity. These questions directly lead to the political debates that do not take place, basically, the determination of the basic functions of the State and the Government and of the necessary country model.

It is difficult to understand that since the founding of the **G-20** group, and even less so from the **G-8**, the abolition of the **57** tax havens currently declared worldwide, when it is in the public domain, has not been requested. purpose of its existence, lies in the accumulation of capital and tax evasion. In other words, the non-contribution, through taxes to the general social good. No head of state has made the proposal over the past century or in the current one. The widespread impunity, probably, is one of the causes of greater social indignation.

Paul Feyerabend, affirms that the model of society is more, and above all a moral problem of the theorists, than a real situation and is solved with common sense. If the future is impossible to predict, it can not be planned and excessive planning entails corruption. This is the reason why the State imposes its tactics violently. The material world, is managed by the ruling elites, the individuals who had to hold the authentic sovereignty, the citizens, receive the designs of power, with the hope put in the faith.

We understand that Feyerabend is right, only in part. Certain predictions of medium range, if they can be made about the future. Lakatos, affirms categorically, that the perception of risk distinguishes what is rational from what is not. Heidegger and Ortega, agree in saying that man is *'futurity'*, a term that involves the vision of the future possibilities, varied and rich and the enormous distance, of those possible ideals with the current situation. There is no brake, except the will, to reach any of the desirable futures.

Edgard Morin, has distinguished between the terms 'globalization' and 'planetarization'. The second term, involves the definition of man as a bio-cultural being, that is, in close relationship with his environment, of which he is a part, and which behaves with respect to it, as sapiens-demens and not as homo sapiens-sapiens.

The vision of its physical continent is reducing, simplifying and, of course, excluding. In parallel, the dual existence of the human being as a physical and metaphysical being, directly damages the planet. In that sense, the trust in the human being, as an entity capable of solving any type of eventuality through technological progress and discovery, has damaged the physical environment of the planet out of disregard. It is again a neoliberal postulate, widely used.

Both cultural and biologist views are necessarily reducing reality. The Spanish ecologist, of greater international relevance, Ramón Margalef, had already warned, after the Second World War, that the relevant unit for really effective analysis and social action was in the 'ecosystem'.

So far, the loss of contact with the past, the forgetting of the place where the human being comes from, was compensated by an indestructible faith in the future.

The anonymization, atomization, commodification, moral degradation and growing discomfort of different societies, progresses independently but in parallel and constantly. The loss of responsibility of the state machinery, fossilized, departmentalized and hyper-specialized and the loss of solidarity and attention of the institutions, with the anonymous being and the marked obsession for money and profit, represent a series of generalized perceptions, that different collectives social, perceive as unacceptable and worthy of participation in contrary alternatives and active response.

Certain predictions made in the past, are being fulfilled for some years. The social movements, ferments of a planetary society, which oppose the general trend of planetary globalization, generating *anthropolitics*, understood as the politics of the human being, regardless of place of origin, ethnicity or belief. Both prosaic pragmatism and abstract reason without empirical contrast directly direct humanity to mythologize self-deception. This is the mythical norm of the neoliberal worldview.

The neoliberal principles, advocate a minimal intervention of the state and absence of restrictions, to the confused individual reality. The social satisfaction in the conception defended by Jeremy Bentham, is opposed to the one defended by Wilfredo Pareto. The first states, that essentially, all people are equal and tend to maximum enjoyment, this would behave, antisocial behavior, as we are seeing in the various corruption schemes and the second author, concludes that the level of maximum social satisfaction is reached when it is not possible to grant any other wealth, to any particular individual without taking it from another individual. It seems that capitalist society has pulverized all limitations. As a well-known socialist policy of our country expressed: "public money belongs to nobody". Regrettable and indecorous.

Chapter XV. A Repeated Scene

> "It governs better who governs less"
>
> - Lao Tse. Chinese philosopher-

> "I think that over time we deserve not to have governments"
>
> José Luis Borges. Argentine writer-

The information processing rules are really simple. Conditioned by the perception of temporal evolution, always in the linear sense, that is, forward, the cause-effect duality is one of the most influential norms of human cognitive functioning. The *'dual thinking'*, acts basically, both by association and by opposition. If two events coincide over time, they tend to associate and often perceive themselves, as the first cause of the second. For this reason, two deferred events in the temporal continuum present greater difficulty in being associated. Likewise, two differentiated facts generate difficulties, to be perceived as caused by the same agent.

Thus, it is difficult to understand that the migration of Syrian refugees, the rebirth of radical movements, of both political senses -right-wing and ultra-left- and the rise of nationalism and independentism, share the same generating principle, which consists in the pressure, first of historical imperialism and later, of capitalism global.

Like any system, the global sociopolitical situation tends to be in a stable situation, which by statistical rule, is identified with the most disorganized state possible. The intervention, through the pressure of an important part of the total system, in this case the US directed towards the maximum territorial and economic expansion, first using the basic strategy of imperialism, consisting of cultural imposition, has historically had different scenarios, but America Latina, it has been its test laboratory par excellence.

However, the countries of clearly differentiated culture and with natural resources, mainly oil and other energy sources, have been addressed through the third phase of imperialism, that is, militarism or armed invasion, as in the case of the countries of the East. Middle and Africa, whose most notable examples have been, Iraq, Syria in the East and Libya in Africa.

The continued war in Syria, produced throughout the area, by the continuous maneuvers of support and demolition of politically convenient governments, has convulsed the area without any historical truce. The migratory phenomenon that we have already described -the migration of Syrian refugees- takes place in this case, due to the impossibility of maintaining personal security and the risk of imminent death. Europe, with its response, has shown that it is really little more than a monetary unit. Philosophical ideals, if they ever existed, have been diluted by the first serious challenge.

Secondly, the constant pressure, in the economic and social areas, mainly dictated by Germany, the austerity measures dictated by the economic Troika, and ultimately by the global financial institutions, have generated a protest reaction, above all, of the younger sectors and better prepared intellectually.

The different tides in our country, the protest of the 15 de Mayo platform and the independence movements, are some of the expected reactions against excessive pressure. The mechanical contraction of the dominant subsistence, also occurs automatically. The use of the legislative, judicial and criminal power is based on the repressive formula, of clearly inadequate effects, of these responses of the reactive systemic components. Thus, in our country, for example, the enactment of the gag law or the judicialization of the Catalan separatist movement are some examples.

While in Europe, the radical parties, especially neo-Nazism, reach levels of social support, never before confirmed. Regionalization in the face of globalization. The economic and social myopia of the political elites, their degree of ignorance, is frankly alarming. Ernesto Sábato, now deceased, expressed with great lucidity his **95** years in **2006** "the patriotism of poor countries, has been called populism or much worse, terrorism."

A complex system experiences typical and general phases, regardless of its nature, social, biological or political, always reacting different subsystems pressed by the dominant subsystem, in an incessant search for stability and balance.

The solutions for systemic *'homeostasis'* or equilibrium, necessarily pass through the introduction of a stabilizing factor of the system or any other element, either structural, or functional, of a nature and significant effects. In that sense, the policies of the established powers must undergo a drastic turn. A sign in that sense, have been the recent statements of the European government of Brussels, in the sense of ending the restrictive economic policies prevailing in the EU.

Previously, the failure and degradation until its practical extinction of the UN, shows the complexity of ordering an international system, modulated by the interests of the most developed and influential nations, specifically the G-8 - United States, Germany, Canada, Japan , United Kingdom, France, Italy and Russia-.

It has manifested repeatedly, and widespread in our country, another phrase expressed, as the disaffection of citizenship with politics. It discourages the ignorance of the supposed political leaders, of socially relevant concepts. The term *'anomìe'*, was already described by Emile Durkheim in the year **1897** and studied by the sociologist Robert K. Merton, in later dates. It is a feeling, characterized by the loss of suppression of values, both moral and religious as well as civic, associated with feelings of alienation, impotence and social indecision.

The loss of such values leads to the infallible destruction of the social order. This characteristic state reflects an individual with fear, anguish, insecurity and dissatisfaction, feelings that lead directly, to unwanted behaviors, among them, divorces and suicides.

The individual perceives suffering as an evil 'infinite'. *Anomy*, is quite common when the social environment, assumes significant changes in economics, for example, either for good or for bad, and more generally, when there is a significant gap between the ideological theories and common values taught and the practice in the daily life.

In response to the global situation, a broad list of reactions to economic and social oppression, derived from economic globalization, can be drawn up. "The Movement of the Landless" -MST- in Brazil, the *Zapatista Army of National Liberation* -EZLN- in Mexico or the World Social Forum (WSF) and the *Peasant way*, at an international level.

Worthy of mention in this section is the huge list of Non-Governmental Organizations -NGO´s- that have emerged, with the ultimate goal of alleviating the inefficiency and lack of operation of governments in the effective management of the basic components of human life, with unwanted results, such as hunger, overcrowding in refugee settlements, medical care, living conditions in general, minimal training of the population, in such essential factors as birth control and a long list.

In **1972,** the NGO is constituted, of greater notoriety of the world, and of more combative spirit. Greenpeace is born, announcing an unstoppable trend, the movement that brings together under the heading of sustainable development, a wide myriad of interests, movements and organizations, before the inoperability of international agreements and the management of formal governments. Numerous organizations have arisen for the treatment of the different problems of global scope. Greenpeace leads the fight for ecology and environmental respect. Doctors Mundi and Doctors without Borders, attends to diseases caused by poverty and lack of attention of third world countries.

Red Cross, constitutes a flag in international solidarity. Save The Children, Intermon-Oxfam, Children Villages, United Hands and a long list of private initiatives, are the protagonists of a struggle, whose causes are economic, but their start and sustenance, responds to principles of character, clearly moral and philosophical. Among the opposition movements to the current global situation, a general movement has arisen, with a marked intellectual component, which brings together a large number of scientific specialties, support platforms and, in reality, represents a current of thought, under the generic label of *sustainable development.*

One of the conclusions established by Dr. Go Harlem Bruntland, author of the report "Our Common Future," was the affirmation that the difference between the poor and the rich, regardless of their goodness or moral condition, was one of the causes of change climate. Most governments either did not understand or did not mind this conclusion.

Actually, the causal sequence is somewhat longer. The countries of the North, condemn the countries of the third world, to a totally extractive productive policy, based on production methods that generate a continuous attack on the environment and the ecosystem in general. That and not another, is the first cause of the truth of the claim, on the inequality, originated by the countries with extractive economies, on the underdeveloped countries. So far, called 'third world countries'. At the present time, there are only countries of the first world and poor countries. The developing countries, which should constitute the 'second world', represent, like many empty terms, a mere entelechy and one of the most shameful euphemisms.

Closely related to the previous point, the appearance of the phenomenon of 'volunteerism' deserves a special mention, both for the objectives it allows to cover, and for the cleanliness and moral height of its millions of components. Channeled and organized, by institutions, organizations, foundations and in their majority, by the own ONG's, they have been distributed by all the planet, allowing to take care of a great number of necessities, that of another way, they had become an unthinkable objective.

The human quality, necessary for the realization of the various actions, which make up the panorama of voluntary action, reaches with frankness, values worthy of praise. Far from being appealed and accused, Western governments, thank and with enormous impudence and impudence, demand and loan volunteering.

The behavior of the EU -European Union- or better of its governments, in the recent crisis of Syrian refugees, is simply despicable, supporting one of the fundamental theses of this document.

The behavior of the national groups and of the nations, in their managerial strata, obeys fundamentally and in a dominant way, to a material and interested criterion, to an economic motivation. The legitimate motivations of government, in particular the service to the community and the achievement of the common good, have simply disappeared. And what is even worse, they are not claimed by the majority. The European Union, far from becoming a bastion of the values legitimized by the French Revolution and which it assumed as its own, has clearly shown that it represents little more than a monetary union.

Some illustrious people of our country, propose as a strategic objective, the European reconstruction. They would do better to undertake in the first place the construction of a new country, at least as a logical and achievable beginning.

Chapter XVI. That Mysterious Character

"Institutions go through three periods: service, privileges and abuse"

-René de Chateaubriand. Diplomat and French writer-

The Club of Rome, was created in the year **1970**, under Swiss legislation, five years before the first oil crisis and these circumstances, do not obey a mere chance. There are serious doubts about its real purpose and its ideological orientation, because, two years before, the Italian leader Arturo Peccei and the Scot, Alexander King, had expressed great concern, expressed in the first working meeting of the group. It focused basically on speculation about the growth of the world population, especially in communist countries, such as China and uncertain future, such as India, which had recently become independent of British rule. They wanted to stop the communist danger, as well as overpopulation.

In order to know the distinctive features of the world situation, they commissioned Dr. Donella Meadows to prepare a report with this objective, which under the title of "the limits of growth", was published in **1972**. The conclusions strike like a blow of gigantic proportions, in the prevailing neocapitalismo, and above all, in its underlying principles, based on the principle of permanent and indefinite progress.

The main conclusions of the report, noted the impossibility of continued growth, according to conceptual and economic guidelines, followed so far, mainly for two reasons. The 'load capacity of the planet' had been surpassed by industrial discharges and the general rates of environmental pollution had skyrocketed.

From that moment, the political ecology emerged, as a discipline of activist orientation and the beginning of the emergence of Non-Governmental Organizations. Dr. Meadows herself, faithful to its principles, has been dedicated for some years to the conception and design of sustainable and self-sufficient cities.

She report had an impact on the birth of different social, political and activist movements of a social nature. The political ecology, the political party of the Greens, *ecofeminism*, environmentalism, as well as in general, Non-Governmental Organizations -ONG´s-, are some of the most significant. From that moment, the Club of Rome has more than **100** specialists from practically all the countries of the world, including the prestigious Spanish economist, Ramón Tamames, and has commissioned the preparation of **21** global reports.

The latest report entitled "2052: A projection for the next 40 years", confirms the predictions and trends established in the Bruntland report - popular name of the first report- and warns, about the urgent need to maintain the global temperature of the planet, below of the presumable increase of **2º** for the next years, mainly due to the disastrous effects it would have on the world as we know it.

One of the practical consequences of the different reports has been the preparation of the climate agenda, a series of international meetings to manage the growing phenomenon of climate change. The summit, held in Rio de Janeiro in **1992**, entitled "the Earth Summit", encouraged well-founded hopes. The resolutions have been systematically breached, mainly due to the veto of the United States of America, the most polluting country in all the industrialized regions, responsible for a **14 %** of the global volume of toxic emissions to the planet's atmosphere. The last climate conference was held in Paris, in the year **2015**, under the auspices of the UN -United Nations- and with the participation of 195 countries. It aims to overcome the 'Kyoto Protocol', signed in **1997** and the agreements reached in the inoperative meeting in Copenhagen in **2007**.

The First World Conference on Climate, organized in Geneva, reserves the merit of considering climate change, for the first time, as a real threat to the planet. The Conference adopted a declaration urging governments to anticipate and avoid possible changes in the climate caused by man. In **1988**, the *'Intergovernmental Panel on Climate Change'* (IPCC) was created, created by the World Meteorological Organization and the *'United Nations Environment Program'*. It was stated that only with strong measures to stop emissions of greenhouse gases would global warming be prevented. That concluded the Group that gathered opinions of approximately 400 scientists, belonging to different specialties. An official response to the threat of climate change began with negotiations at the United Nations, in the 1990s in a group that would eventually become the *United Nations Convention on Climate Change (*UNCCD).

To date, this group has presented four evaluation reports on climate change, including the description and approaches offered by science, of the phenomenon studied, as well as their possible future impacts and viable solutions.

Exposed in chronological order for better understanding, the first was organized in **1992**, the United Nations Conference on Environment and Development -popularly known as the Earth Summit in Rio de Janeiro, Brazil -. World leaders adopted the plan known as *'Schedule 21'*, an ambitious program of action, for global sustainable development.

Its areas of activity were basically oriented towards the fight against climate change, the protection of biodiversity and the elimination of toxic substances emitted into the biosphere. Its entry into force dates back to **1994**, after having received the necessary number of ratifications by the different countries that participated in the Conference. In **1995** the *´First Conference of the Parties´* -COP- was organized in Berlin -Germany-.

After this signature, the group of nations that have signed the UNFCCC, has met annually. The signing of the *'Kyoto Protocol'* is considered the effective starting point of the fight against climate change. The industrialized countries acquired concrete commitments and a timetable for action. The binding agreement establishes a reduction of **5.2%** in emission of greenhouse gases, for the period between the years **2008-2012**. The objective to date, has not been achieved.

The last and fourth report, corresponding to the year **2007**, was prepared by about **600** authors from **40** countries, and reviewed by **620** experts and representatives of the different world governments. The work of the IPCC has been recognized as a global scientific consensus by the national science academies of various countries. In **2007** he shared the Nobel Peace Prize with Al Gore, -ex-American vice president-.The reaction of civil society, became highly critical, if it was not already previously. The pressures on governments and meetings in the industrialized countries narrowed.

In the year **2007**, in Bali, the negotiation process of the industrialized countries was restarted, for the achievement of the second phase of the objectives, set for the period **2012-2020**. A road map -*Bali Road Map*- was established, focused on three generic objectives: the mitigation of emissions, the necessary technological adaptation and the financing of these initiatives.

The results obtained would be evaluated at the ´Copenhagen Conference´, held in **2009**. It was again fixed, the generic goal, not to exceed the 2º warming limit, but no mention was made of the way to achieve it. The ´Cancun Conference´ of the year **2010** created the '*Green Climate Fund*', with the objective of providing financing for projects and activities in developing countries. The ´*Durban Conference*´ followed, in its **XVII** edition of ´*Conferences on Climate Change*´. So far, countless meetings, zero performances.

The behavior of the industrialized countries, manifests a programmatic and classic mode of action, based on agreeing and not carrying out any practice, against economic interests, based on massive and polluting productivist practices.

The Kyoto agreement, still not produced, despite its irreparable short-term climatic consequences. According to the resolution passed in Durban, the main emitters of greenhouse gases, such as the United States. and the newly industrialized countries, Brazil, China, India and South Africa are willing to initiate a process, which would be completed in year **2015** and which should conclude, with a binding agreement, on climate protection.

At present, the resolutions are not being applied, mainly because of the repeated veto of the United States, the world's largest producer by far, of the emission of industrial pollutants and CO_2 into the atmosphere. It will soon be **45** years since the first report of the Club of Rome was drawn up. Not only the situation has not changed, it has worsened in a proportion that has already reached an asymptotic level, that is, maximum.

Chapter XVII. What a Beautiful Landscape

All forms of government are valued exclusively to the extent that they tend to promote the happiness of those who live under them.

-Adam Smith. Philosopher and Scottish economist-

The Earth since its formation, **4,500** million, along with the rest of the galaxy, has undergone profound changes, both due to internal causes, such as volcanic eruptions and glaciations and external, mainly due to impacts of asteroids of various sizes. The general rule has consisted in an adaptation of the general conditions of the planet before the change, independently of the type of cause that has caused the change.

As a computer of global dimensions, it has modified and adapted its main conditions, showing itself as a unique and interconnected super-system. This is so, to the point that some pseudo-religious movement has developed the concept of *'Gaia'*, considering the planet as an immense living and intelligent organism, with unsuspected response capabilities and its own aims and objectives, consisting of its survival and own development. This myth coincides with the previous pre-Columbian belief, reigning in the Central and South American civilizations, of the global divine entity, called *Pachamama*.

From the temporary beginning, and by different factors combined, the planet has passed from an ignition stage, to generate more stable conditions, mainly due to the appearance of the atmosphere, sufficient for the appearance of complex life.

A certain distance to the source of galactic heat, a medium-sized star -the Sun- has allowed to maintain the global temperature, in a favorable arc for the appearance of life, even though the Sun, provides a 1000 times greater energy of the necessary for the existence and due to the atmospheric protection, the harmful radiations -like the gamma rays-, are neutralized, by that harmonic shield.

In a simple million years, the homo sapiens, has gone from the culture of fire to the realization of space travel, and only a space of 250,000 years, which ended the last great glaciation, originated the great civilizations.

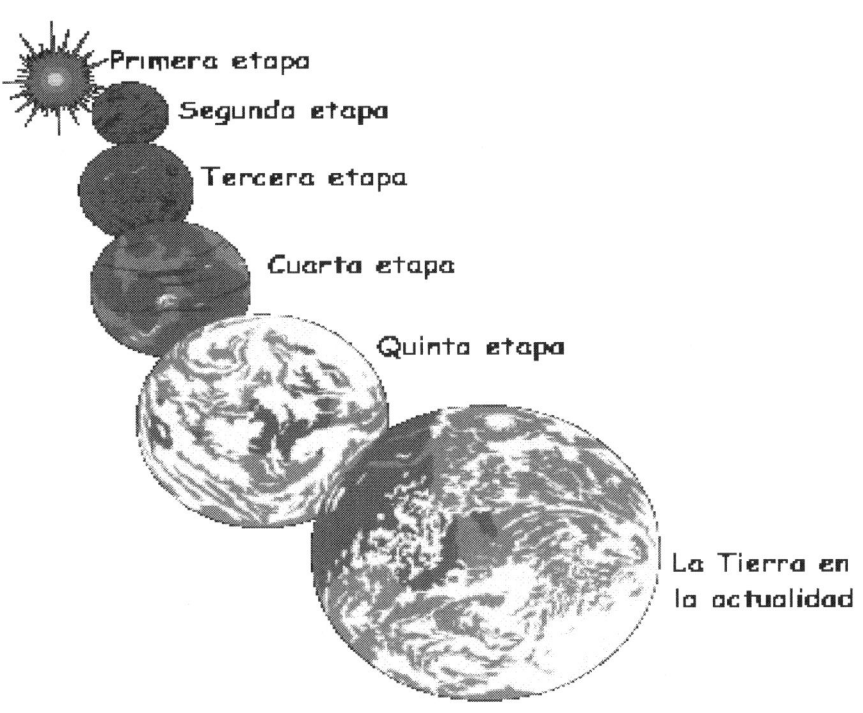

The planet Earth has undergone great transformations since its formation approximately 4,500 million years ago. Impacts of asteroids, tectonic movements, glaciations or volcanic eruptions. As an interconnected macro-system has generated new configurations, one of which allowed the development of intelligent life. The most likely reaction to the marked climate change produced by human activity will be a process of destabilization and global warming whose consequences can be disastrous and irreversible.

The state of technology, coinciding with the evolution of scientific thought and a determined ideological substratum, neoliberalism and its unwavering conviction in the belief of unlimited progress, have developed a productive system, with extractive orientation, that generates probably irrecoverable consequences, in the environmental environment. The main symptoms are diverse and deep-seated; hunger and poverty, environmental impact, devastating, depletion of non-renewable energies, overpopulation, climate change, global warming and contamination of basic ecosystems.

At the moment of describing, the cited consequences, must preside over the analysis, the systemic axiom, that all the subsystems of the planet, are deeply interconnected and in addition to this, that the progress of the deterioration does not obey the linear logic, of an additive or summative nature, but on the contrary, it is governed by the exponential, multiplicative logic of the effects.

However, in order to follow a comprehensible sequence, the cycle that causes climate change can start, with the process of desertification of the planet. A central and decisive milestone, begins with the indiscriminate felling of the Amazon forest, led by logging companies, during the past century, mainly. The Amazon, has been cataloged as the "lung of the planet". The forest absorbs a large amount of carbon dioxide during the day- one of the main agents that cause the greenhouse effect -releasing oxygen during the night. At the time of exposing more soil to solar radiation, a deterioration begins in the upper layers of the soil itself. One of the many vicious circles in the climate begins.

The vegetation, in its emission to the atmosphere of oxygen, generates the clouds that produce the subsequent rain. Its disappearance causes a lower amount of precipitation, preventing the effect of the planet's refreshment and contributing even more to the progressive desertification.

When there is more soil, which absorbs solar radiation, the thermal effect of heat increases the global temperature. Global warming constitutes a fundamental part of the generalized climate change.

Continuing with the chain of interconnected events, the progressive increase in temperature affects the geographic and magnetic poles of the planet, where the largest amount of ice is concentrated. The Arctic pole, above all, but in the same way, the Antarctic pole, progressively melts. Another one of the vicious circles begins, added -it must not be forgotten- to the previous one. The loss of frozen mass, by its white color, acts as an immense reflector of the solar rays, maintaining the planetary temperature. The greater the amount of ice that disappeared, the greater the increase in temperature. The 2º limit, mentioned above, would produce a level of melting of the Antarctic ice mass, which would pour water into the ocean mass.

The level of the oceans would consequently increase. A rise of **50 cms.** Above the current level, drastically change the known coastal profile and affect the configuration of all coastal cities today, leading to the partial collapse and in some cases total of some locations, whose most obvious case is the city of Venice.

One more variation, should be added to climate changes. The current of 'El Niño' is a marine current, of warm character and with a marked seasonality, typical of Ecuador and that takes place annually, in the Pacific Ocean. It moves in a North to South direction, reaching the Ecuadorian coasts, in the month of December. The effects of warm waters for crops are highly beneficial, as it also affects the biological cycle of the equatorial forest. However, in recent years, the increase in temperature in the current, has resulted in a phenomenon, which causes a greater proportion of rainfall, causing floods and another series of natural disasters, due to radical climate change.

The next stage, derived from the massive industrial process, is found in the toxic spills, to both basic systems of the planet: water and soil. Industrial waste, which ends in rivers and seas, affects the natural flow of rainwater. They influence, therefore, in the fresh water deposits of the soil, natural aquifers and natural water currents. The irrigation of crops is automatically contaminated. But it did not stop, the cultivated food, suffer intoxication that in a later phase, are destined for human consumption. The presence of heavy metals can not be eliminated naturally by the body. Inland waters, also contaminated with mercury, nickel, copper and lead, in different quantities, are ingested by fish. The alarm about livestock consumption has had global repercussions. At present, it extends to fish intended for human consumption.

The third chapter of climate change, refers directly to global warming. The emissions of gases, especially CO_2 into the atmosphere, constitute the decisive element in the increase of planetary warming. They cause the so-called 'greenhouse effect', since the existence of the atmosphere, does not let pass the gases generated in the biosphere, the cold body that forms the outer space. Machinism -whose maximum exponent is the automobile- is another manifestation of the industrialist archetype.

The gases generated by the combustion in automobiles, from fossil fuels, mainly oil, are the main source of greenhouse gas emissions into the atmosphere. Obviously, the solution does not go through the abolition of the automobile. But yes, by the rationalization of its use and of the advisable general practice, of the abandonment of polluting energies and the development of the group of clean and renewable.

The current development of some of them, is frankly promising. In close connection with this point, we must mention the permanence of nuclear power plants, a priority energy option in the energy sector. Obviating the consequences generated by the known disasters of Chernobyl and Japan, they have existed in other countries, such as Canada or Spain. Air emissions of known carcinogenic power elements, especially dioxins, heavy metal leaks, contribute to the contamination of basic systems. Model countries, admired by the neoliberal ideology, such as Germany, abandoned the use of nuclear energy in the past century.

The inaction or failing that, the delay in the institutional response, to the consequences generated by the application of the neoliberal economic system, by national and global institutions, has led, in addition to the active opposition, methodological criticisms, to the sustaining principles of the neo-capitalist economic model, coming from the intellectual spearhead of the sustainable development movement. The greatest criticisms have been directed to the assessment of the suitability and conceptual efficacy, underlying the general assumptions on which traditional economy is based; in its most basic approaches.

The first and fundamental, is directed to the denial of the ideological basis, implicit in the criteria used, for measuring the growth of societies. It also entails relevant methodological flaws. Two clear examples are represented by the usual indices in the assessment of national economic growth. In the first place, the average *per capita* income, which is used from the governmental and, what is worse, economic levels, constitutes a methodological fallacy, of a dimension that is hardly credible. The average is a statistical measure of central tendency, which is neither operative nor adequate, when the dispersion of the distribution, in this case, of the economic rent, is very broad.

Expressed in simple words, it is not adequate because there is a minority of population, which has a very high level of economic resources and a large majority, whose income is very scarce and above all, the distance between both groups is very large.

In addition, the middle class, which could contribute as a social justification, to statistical error, is disappearing. The most appropriate measure would be fashion, which, in its quantifiable meaning, represents the range of subjects with the greatest representation. A clear example is observed in the setting of the average salary. If the average is used, in our country, this index would be above **1200** euros. On the other hand, if fashion is used, as a valid statistical index, it is below the minimum inter-professional salary, that is, less than **700** euros. The consideration of the median, that is to say, of the position that is right in the middle of the distribution, would also help to a more adjusted understanding of the economic reality.

Likewise, the use of the *'Gross Domestic Product'* -GDP- as the only measure of the growth of the national economy is criticized with increasing force, and this, for a double reason. Its internal construction, obeys to an equation or better, mathematical algorithm, of equivocal sense, at least. When dealing with purely numerical data, qualitative aspects are not taken into account, such as the desirability or social desirability of the factors considered. For example, some economic technicians have denounced the scarce real representativeness of GDP, since it does not include economic flows, which are found in social reality, such as prostitution or drug trafficking.

In addition, and continuing with the illustrative examples, if an epidemic or pandemic occurs, as it happens in a large part of the African countries, the government's health expenditure increases remarkably. This expense would have an impact on the increase in the gross domestic product, when from any point of view, undesired and undesirable growth results.

Some theorists of sociological and also economic origin, have proposed the use of two added criteria. The first of these has been defined as the Population Welfare Index. This indicator, would collect the perceptions and symptoms of social groups, fundamentally, showing itself as an equivalent, to the quality of life or vital counterpoint, of the mere general economic indicators. In other words, and as has happened in our country, the drop in the price of oil, coupled with the decision of the president of the European Central Bank, Mario Draghi, to acquire public debt from different European countries, has enabled an improvement in macroeconomic indicators.

These and not the government's performance in economic matters, have been the cause of the positive macroeconomic figures, of the growth of the last two years. In addition to this, the growing tourism, due in part to the loss of inflow of traditional destinations, located in areas of armed conflict, mainly in the African continent and the Near East, have contributed to an economic improvement, as we say, in the great economic indicators.

But the persistence of poverty suffers a continuous increase, denounced by different non-governmental organizations and also by political and economic analysts. It should appear, in the social dialectic and above all politics, an indicator of the quality of life of citizens and their perceived degree of adequacy. In a similar sense, it has been proposed, the consideration of a *'Total Happiness Index'*. The meaning and objectives of this indicator is similar to the previous one.

Critics from sustainability theorists, have grouped under the rubric of a relatively new concept, the irreparable damage caused to the ecosystem environment. The *'ecological footprint'* refers to the environmental damage that human civilization, in its desperate predatory desire, has shaped on the planet. The reduction, not only, of the non-renewable natural resources, but above all, the insurmountable transgression, of the carrying capacity of the biosphere as a whole, which, as its name indicates, consists of the planetary levels, in which the lifetime. In addition to this, or rather, as a direct consequence, one of the irremovable principles laden with logical weight of sustainability is pulverized.

It refers to equity or inter-generational justice. The voracity of the planetary inhabitants of the present, has mortgaged and even more ruined, the ecological capital, the natural rents, that by own right, had the future generations. Our descendants and the children of our children.

Chapter XVIII. The Specialized Criticisms

> "So that the one who believes does not need any explanation: for the one who does not believe every explanation remains"
>
> -Franz Werfel. Novelist, poet and Austrian dramatist-

Criticisms of savage hegemonic capitalism and the underlying neoliberal ideology are so numerous that they must be grouped by categories to facilitate their evaluation. The first of these, by its own tradition of the discipline from which it comes, ethics, as a fundamental part of philosophy, becomes a conceptual disaster for neocapitalism. It is appropriate to indicate, only as anecdotal data, that the fundamental work of Marx, "The Capital" has increased its sales by **800 %** since the beginning of the last economic crisis

Beyond the insignificant detail, Schumpeter, one of the most prestigious economists of the past century, in his most famous work, exposes in a simple way, the criticism of some of the basic postulates of neoliberal international capitalism. In the purely economic order, the basic ideology is obsessively directed to the fulfillment of the principle, enunciated as the *'profits maximalization'*. Perhaps, with depth and moral depth, it shows an endogenous attitude in its ideology -and also necessary for the achievement of its purposes-, of disregard for the other, the different and also, the desire for public appearance, for ostentation of power. An undeniable sign in the domain over others.

At this point, it is worth adding another of the economic-social principles, which are derived from the predatory yearning of capitalism, such as the *'socialization of losses and the privatization of profits'*. The transfer towards private ownership of all economic activity generating profit focus, has become a haunting banner of neoliberalism, and constantly agitated in any way and anywhere.

In our country, the privatization of public health represents a clear and hurtful example. This fact, indeed, is linked to the strong feeling of contempt for any other person not belonging to their self-defined social class, and of course, to the sum of them, that is, the mass. The contempt on the part of the dominant elites is greater, insofar as it has a double motive. It is despised by the consideration of inferior and because it needs your collaboration, as an indispensable producer of work and wealth. The supremacy with respect to the rest, builds a permanent wall and for this same reason, endogenous and immovable.

The fundamental criticisms, in the conceptual section, refer to the unacceptable falsity of the ideological principle of unlimited progress. Spoliation of non-renewable resources continues, so that Kenneth Boulding said the fact with the phrase "who defend the idea of unlimited progress or else a madman or an economist". The aggregation of natural resources to capital, that is, their consideration as free of any rate, becomes a theoretical error of the utmost gravity and extensive consequences. The creation of financial bubbles, the feeling that the crisis is localized and comes from abroad, are presuppositions of a degree of absolute falsity.

In that sense, Baran affirms, that capitalism and imperialism are inseparable, condition and necessity, cause and symptom, dysfunction and behavior.

But the critics of greater intellectual depth, are directed towards the central nucleus of the conception of the neocapitalista system. The conceptualization of the market system as an autonomous entity, self-regulating and despise both society which feeds such as state intervention, which should regulate it.

The diversion of funds towards financial capitalism, the use of military force and the cold war, are two added criticisms. The analysis of North American hegemonic and monopoly capitalism, and now global, necessarily implies policies of social inequality, because it regulates the level of deficit, which directly affects public spending on social services. This rule is found in the bases of the agreements of the granting of loans by the World Bank and the IMF, to all the countries to which they are granted, even today.

The exploitation of the so-called mono-culture *economies*, that is, of most of the riches of the underdeveloped countries, an industrial exercise of the world monopoly and the policy of loans, which constitute the external debt of these countries, entails the fact that historically, no external debt has been satisfied, and this due to a double motive. The increase of constant interest and its use as a weapon of economic dependence.

The fall of socialism, existing until the year **1989**, has worsened the global panorama, since at this moment, the Chinese economy -also with communist ideology-, has become incomprehensibly, in an ally and investor of the North American economy. While the Americans spend, supported by a difficult quantifiable external debt, the Chinese population, saves and saved capital, is invested in the US economy to allow a consumerist and productivist debauchery of a schizoid nature.

The methodology and philosophy of the neoliberal framework is revealed, perhaps, as its most characteristic feature. The centers of power, both legitimate and legal, are allied to extract the resources of the great mass of the population. The average citizen projects a constant flow of economic resources to the extractive system, implanted in a coercive way. The collection channels for resources are established by the government, through taxes, both direct and indirect.

This condition has the necessary character of obligatory nature. Non-compliance automatically goes to the administrative sanction or, in the worst case, criminal. Industrial corporations and banking entities, prevalent tools of the commercial oligopoly, extract resources, not by means of mandatory taxation, but through strategies of a higher level of sophistication, such as the creation of new needs, the identification of different products with signs of distinction or social class and also by ineffective and sometimes deceptive products. The policy of price agreements emerges as a usual practice in practically all sectors of commercial activity, and even more so in the sectors of first necessity.

Energy companies, such as power companies or gas stations -owned by big oil companies- are some examples. Another case, with unaffordable moral background, focuses on corporations in the pharmaceutical sector. This type of companies, do not intend to cure diseases, but only treat the symptom of the disease. Otherwise, your big business would end. Against all odds, they only dedicate a tiny percentage of their turnover to the research and development activity.

In the second place, a usual commercial tactic relies on setting prices, multiplying its production costs by 1000. Sobaldi, the drug necessary for the treatment of hepatitis C, follows this rule. It represents for the sick another different form, of death by poverty.

The government adduces not to distribute the drug, precisely its high price. These added factors configure the true essence of neoliberal intentionality: His extractive nature. The extraction by established channels of the economic resources of the population. Acemoglou and Robinson, have labeled this fact perfectly, through the epigraph of *'extractive'*.

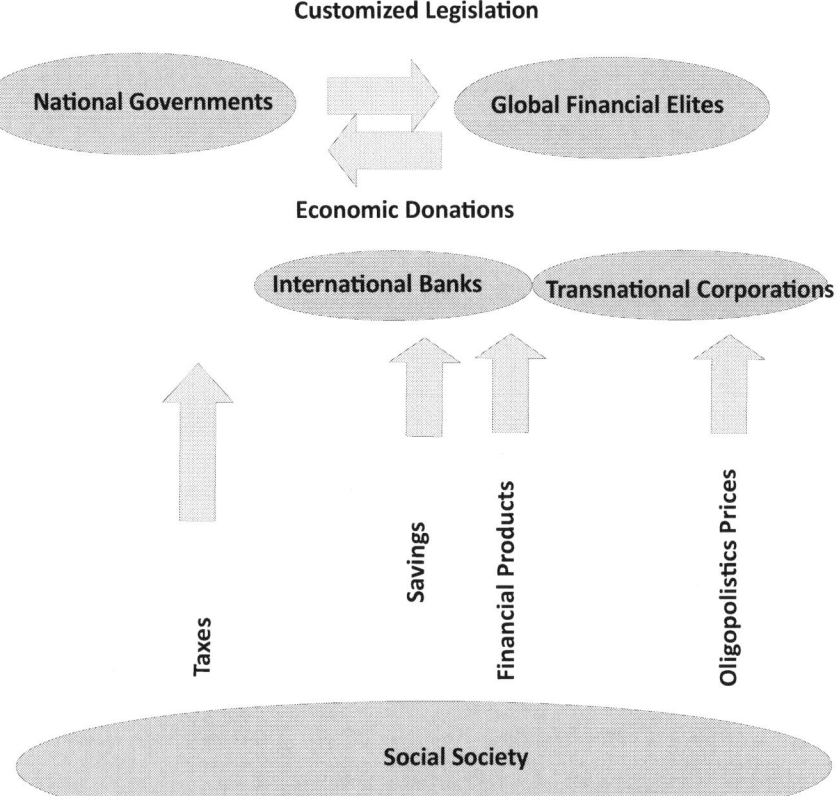

Extractive process of the civil society through the factual powers of the States financed and directed by the global financial Elite. Note the three great ways of collecting the economic resources of the social base. Through taxes, savings and consumption, these last two sources of much greater economic volume. For this reason, the international financial power buys legal provisions and finances the action of the government. Criminal practices and corruption form constitute the legalized business and economic practice.

The extractive intentionality of government structures and the two main types of financial configuration, banks and large commercial corporations, have, for civil society as a whole, lethal consequences in their daily lives.

The big banks, not only facilitate savings, through deposits destined for this purpose. They issue financial products that, given the ethereal nature of the financial investment, are totally fraudulent. This is the case in our country, of the preferred obligations, issued by a merger of savings banks. The necessary institutional complicity of the government, represented in this case, by the Bank of Spain and the National Securities Market Commission, acts in connivance, for the general objective of the plundering of private savings. In this type of common action, if it can be applied appropriately, the use of the slogan present in the political discourse of *'for the general good'*. General of private interests.

No less scandalous and fraudulent, the oligopolistic practices of large companies appear, operating in strategic sectors, such as those corresponding to energy and fuel. The electric companies, in our country, have increased in percentages that oscillate around **30 %** annual, the price of the electric power, under unsustainable pretexts. Likewise, oil companies increase fuel prices at the time of rising prices at source, but instead, do not act consistently, otherwise, the decrease in the price of fuel, as the current. The price of fuels never suffers significant decreases. The complicity of the governmental institutions in both cases is economically compensated with sufficiency, through illegal donations to political parties, which support the National Governments by the industrial consortiums.

The excessive and continued pressure on the social mass, produces a remarkable and necessary reaction of the social collective, which, through structures organized to a greater or lesser degree, generates protest movements, both against governments and institutions, and against representative institutions of global economic power. Popular demonstrations, general strikes and work stoppages exemplify the first group; the one corresponding to the opposition to the national powers.

The international anti-capitalist and environmentalist movements are present in the economic summits and world economic assemblies, such as the Davos World Economic Forum and personalize the world protest, this time, against the world leaders of the global capitalist movement.

The social response has no passing or casual characteristics. It is about the use of a mode of action, which has made it possible to achieve significant improvements in the social struggle, which represents a historical constant. Anti-protest laws and the use of police action do not seem sufficient to contain them. The suffrage movements in the past and human rights, at present, already enjoy international notoriety.

The savage capitalist system does not support a rigorous examination, in any of the categories of socioeconomic valuation. On a purely economic level, such practices become a constant generator of poverty and inequality, both intro-country and inter -country. The countries that are under its operation, are impoverished progressively, due to the accumulation of capital in a small group of people and companies, and the distances with the poorest groups, increase.

In other words, the rich are progressively richer and the poor groups, increasingly neglected and evicted. In our country, the number of new millionaires, emerged during the crisis, has grown by **14 %**, while according to data from international organizations, approximately **30 %** of the population is on the line of absolute poverty.

The UN has established degrees of poverty. That has been his best contribution to the global crisis. Recognize and classify widespread poverty. Other organizations such as ECLAC -Economic Commission for Latin America and the Caribbean- and the UNDP -United Nations Development Program- have developed, in the so-called *'Regional Program for the Overcoming of Poverty'* -PRSP-, an ambitious agenda of work.

The two methodological lines of action are directed to the intervention in the poverty line and added to this, the work route directed towards the coverage of the so-called NBI -Basic Basic Needs-. Both methodologies of action, start from an absolute concept of poverty, which one measures in terms of income and the other, in terms of characteristics of goods and services, which the population can access.

In this classification, grade **1** does not have access to coverage of basic needs, such as food or drinking water. Grade **2** lives in conditions of insufferable human overcrowding. Grade **3** does not have access to basic services, much less to the acquisition of necessary tools. And so on.

Different statistical indexes have been developed for estimating and studying global poverty. The first significant conclusion, highlights that more than **1,000** million people, currently live with less than 1 dollar a day, approximately, **15 %** of the world population.

This population lives or better, survives, in depressed areas, mainly in Asia, Latin America and Africa. But the geographical analysis of the deprivation of needs is totally misleading. Poverty exists in a dramatically contrasted way in the countries of the first world. Countries qualified as developed. In Spain and with different degrees of implementation, according to communities and regions, the same data indicate a poverty index of **21.2 %** of the total population of our country.

Some supporters of the neoconservative ideology, argue that governments, assume an excessive challenge, in the attempt to achieve the utopian welfare state. The response that arises automatically, as counter-argument, is easily understandable, overwhelming in its simplicity. If it is not the responsibility of governments, whose demand is it? Who is responsible for transferring the claim? However, in the United Kingdom, different shared initiative projects have worked reasonably effectively. PPP programs- Public Private Programs-.

The different western governments, including Spanish, design and implement rescue programs for institutions, but not for people or groups of citizens and not only those qualified as at risk of social exclusion. The Spanish bank rescue has not been such. Private banking has been consistent in the critical period. The rescue has been directed to the Savings Banks, a model close to the social service at its birth and later, adulterated by the presence on their boards of directors, of political and institutional representatives. The bank rescue, kindly set at **60,000** million, will never be returned to the citizens. This is one of those occasions, in which we would like the prediction to be wrong. We would sincerely wish to be wrong.

The results of all complex systems become consequences and results, characterized by ambivalence or paradox. Also, the global neo-capitalist system. The over-accumulation, generates concentration of capital, power, wealth and knowledge, but destroys businesses, jobs, infrastructure and culture. The use of the peripheral countries, as wells of extraction of resources and fishing grounds of illegal employment, close to slavery, in theory already overcome, faces the offensive, child exploitation, by the large multinationals, which show a friendly public image , in its advertising communications, aimed at the upper economic classes.

The much desired investment of foreign capital, coveted by governments and economic agents and qualified as one of the engines of economic development, is another factor of social pressure and direct cause of the accumulation of various capital gains and facilitating the concentration of large volumes of capital, at the expense of damaging, and also irretrievably, the internal savings capacities of nations.

Neoliberal philosophy and methodology, cause relations of domination and inequality, both from a national perspective, and in the international relationship. Developing countries participate as suppliers of raw materials and cheap labor according to the needs of global production chains, in exchange for violating their internal savings capacities. The chain of global over-exploitation, devours figures known and differentiated until now, such as the peasant, the unequal female employment, the informal or submerged economy, the unproductive effort, the child and forced exploitation. In his immense wisdom, he has managed to create a new massive phenomenon, the 'poor salary', in addition to definitively breaking, the biological chain established by the environmental ecosystem, producer of natural resources, in addition to the climatic conditions necessary for its production.

But the extraction of resources adds another element in the action plan. Once, the productive economies have become impoverished, they are forced, either directly or indirectly, to these countries to resort to the international financial system. The application for loans for development and its permanent submission to the unlimited debt, both in time and in magnitude. The degrees of abuse and disregard multiply. Doubly victimizes poor countries. It has followed, unfailingly, the established principle that "there is no policy, no economy." Obvious statement, in the present economic configuration, but again wrong. The economy is justified by and is creation of, human beings.

The control of large transnational corporations in industrial production, agriculture and services, produces concentration and transfer of wealth, concentration and destruction of capital and concentration of income and expansion of poverty, in addition to their corporate operations, devastate the environment environment since, its requirements in terms of quantity -as much as possible- and time -as little as possible- threaten the capacity for renewal, natural matter, and result in pollution, devastation, erosion, and progressive deterioration.

Most of the time, it causes irreversible damage, which not only damages the environment, but also disrupts the so-called social metabolism, the necessary binomial, man-nature. One of the con-substantial features of neoliberal capitalism, although not the only one, is oriented towards social unsustainability.

Another of the false constitutive principles of the neo-capitalist creed rests on the concept of economic cycle. According to this hypothesis, the world economy experiences cycles, which in a moment lead to the crisis, but within the nature of capitalism, there are mechanisms to revive economic growth.

This is not true, for various reasons, which show that the economic implosion is due to genetic causes, structural deficiency of the system.

The fall in the rate of profit, experienced in total terms, causes a bankruptcy in the process of valorization, that is to say, of the necessary revaluation of the total economic system, which interrupts the dynamics of financing, investment, production, commercialization and growth of the entirety of the system. The world capitalist operating group experiences a crisis of multidimensional meaning, reflected in the economic, social and environmental, and urgently demands a complete change of conceptual system. Western society faces a structural and systemic crisis of great magnitude that puts in predicament the process of social metabolism man-nature and threatens the sources of social wealth.

In terms of greater technical content, the theorists of the economic cycle, find serious difficulties to explain the mechanical trajectory of capital, so that unsuccessfully, expect a *expansive wave* in world trade. From the world-system and the geopolitical analysis, a series of severe circumstances is anticipated. Among them, the collapse of the United States, as a global hegemonic power and the advent of a new era commanded, by a great power, such as the European Union or Japan, or by emerging powers such as Brazil, Russia, India and, mainly, China.

However, the necessary global change requires, as a first condition, the dismantling of the programmatic principles of neo-capitalist action. Perhaps, the main one, is represented by the idea, of the existing prototype, about the misused term *'crisis'*. The current crisis is not a conjuncture or an externality. 'The crisis that comes from outside' is a *'collateral effect'* or a *'localized problem'* -in the United States- or *'sectored'* - financial crisis-.

From our perspective, it is not only a crisis of capital appreciation, but also the deterioration of the economic, social and environmental bases that underpin the totality of neoliberal ideology. That is to say, it is a crisis of the strategy of restructuring and neoliberal expansion, which is presented as a general crisis of world capitalism, the third of its kind, after those that occurred in the decades of the **1930´s** and **1970´s.**

From this position of mostly systemic approach, although it is admitted, that the big capital and the State, try to star in the application of rescue policies, it is clear, and it is relatively simple to predict that, these actions, aggravate and above all, delay, the advent of new and perhaps deeper crises. The only real solution would be a structural and systemic change, a new civilization. However, we must recognize, along with other critics, that at present, there is no alternative social or collective agent, capable of confronting the power of big capital and its operative agents, which make up the so-called *'global imperialism'*.

The predominant analysis of the contemporary crisis, and the consequent corrective actions, are oriented to the preservation of the capitalist system and to the rescue, of the great capitals. The dominant neoliberal vision presents globalization as a global phenomenon, inevitable, without alternatives, and which must be assumed as a challenge. To do this, we must open markets, offer suitable conditions for foreign investment and face the challenge of competitiveness, in which the State must draw the defining conditions of a business-friendly climate, particularly for large multinational corporations, to reduce the labor force, transfer public resources to the private sector, in addition to implementing, a strategy of selling the cities and the territory, where the interests of capital prevail, and not those of the population.

This type of policy is applied, indistinctly, by governments of the right, center-left and left, except for some exceptions, encrypted in governments that try to resist neoliberalism and execute policies that can be designated under the concept of radical nationalism. From this conception, the current crisis of capitalism is considered financial or application of neoliberal policy, so that the State can play a more active role, to reverse the recessive cycle of the economy and recompose the course.

Among the policies proposed, of neo-Keynesian style, the rescue of companies is contemplated, or better, corporations, although it is more of businessmen, not of jobs, nor debtors of the popular classes. However, the phenomenon of globalization, which seems to adopt all the characteristics of a phenomenon that has come to stay, is not put into question.

In general terms, it can easily be verified that the categories of explanations about the current crisis lead to three paradigmatic aspects. The first, groups the *'conventional'* or orthodox vision, from the neoclassical and neoliberal perspective, with the application of the logic of the single thought, and relies on the idea that the crisis is a localized, sectorized and short-term phenomenon with the mitigating factor that their response raises the rescue of big money from the state, regardless that this provision contravenes its neoconservative ideology, but without this, it means a confession part on the invalidity of their political propaganda.

The second, which brings together the *'heterodox perspective'* which receives the positions and Social neo-Keynesian, ie covers the political spectrum center-left, but have common ground, in the characterization of the crisis, with the dominant view, in the sense that it is a localized phenomenon, sectorized and conjunctural.

The difference lies only in that it places responsibility in the neoliberal deregulation and in the greed of the financiers, for which it demands the implementation of new regulations and a greater participation of the State in the tasks of promoting development. Expressed in another way, although it promulgates a nuanced criticism of neoliberalism, it does not question the foundations of capitalism. His proposal, in any case, aims to rescue or reform neoliberal capitalism.

The third analytical side represents the quintessential 'critical view' and characterizes the crisis, from different angles, and structural, systemic and civilizational besides that ascribe attributes whole, multidimensionality and permanence.

The current crisis has been attributed to certain facts, but not enough. The securitization of capital in its search for immediate over-profits and the commercialization of securities and junk bonds, and the free movement of transnational capital and sovereign bonds, represent, in effect, individual causes.

The financialization of the economy acquires global repercussions and destroys any logical principle of the chain production, work and consequent consumption. The planetary economy has been monetized. This fact basically means the continuous diversion of resources destined to the production of goods and services, which provide salaries to the labor force, for its later return to the economic circuit, for the capital destined for speculative investment, which provides a greater performance or profit. This fact, although denounced by the European fashion economist, Piketty, had already been known since the end of the **19th** century.

The financing thesis of the world economy, competes directly, with other alternative explanations. The clear obsession with overproduction identifies a contradiction between the overflowing productive capacity of big capital and the policy of lowering labor, which leads to the decline of demand, in a crisis of realization, of the system itself, as Katz explains.

For a plethora of analysts, neoliberalism is in crisis, due to its congenital inability, to generate sustained growth and human development, and also represents the failure of structural adjustment policies and capitalist institutions headed by the IMF. International Monetary -, WB -World Bank- and WTO -World Trade Organization-. Although neoliberalism, as a "class project", gives good results, in its purpose of concentrating capital, power and wealth in a few hands.

The international financial system collapsed, during the current crisis, to the point where credit, among the segments and instances of financial capital, was soon immobilized. The capitalist expansion has implemented an enormous production capacity, derived from the expansion of global productive chains, and supported by the incorporation of abundant cheap natural resources and the surplus of cheap labor force.

However, one of the supports of this expansive boom has consisted in the containment and real decrease of wages, which has had repercussions in a collapse of mass consumption capacity. This clearly resulted in a crisis of realization. The merchandise cluster had no imminent exit in the market via consumption. The recourse to credit stimulated consumption at the time, but soon succumbed, under the inevitable rules of financialization.

The current situation, is presented as a global economic depression, because it means a colossal fracture of the processes of financing, investment, production, growth and distribution, which besides causing a fall in the rate of profit, brings with it a crisis of realization and a complex process of capital destruction - concentration and centralization of capital.

It has expanded the orbit of the market, privatization, exploitation of cheap labor and environmental devastation, but it has done so at the cost of depressing wages, dismantling the subsistence economy, canceling or diminishing support for the social economy. The result has been a deterioration of mass consumption, thanks to the cheapening of labor and the proliferation of massive defaulted credit, and an abundance of merchandise, without potential buyers.

But even more, the desire to expand profit margins has deteriorated the material conditions of life and work of the majority of the population. To the extent that human life and human dignity can be cataloged, as a disposable resource and, of course, replaceable. The expansion of neoliberal capitalism and the centralized accumulation regime have created a propensity for recurrent crises in different regions of the planet, particularly in the peripheral world.

With this same purpose, the wars unleashed by the imperialist countries, in countries and zones of the periphery, have also appeared, with the purpose of appropriating exclusive and dominant of vast natural resources, such as oil in the case of Iraq, or to overthrow or persuade opposition political regimes, with geostrategic influence. As a correlate, a destructive dynamic of companies, jobs, populations, ecosystems and cultures has been generated.

Peripheral countries have been obligated participants, of the process of financialization through the channeling of profits and diverse types of funds that augured quick and high financial gains to the detriment of the real economy.

We have described in the previous section, the most predatory face of neocapitalism, around renewable and non-renewable natural resources, that is, environmental capital. The multiple consequences of neoliberal ideology and practice, acquire from any perspective, global dimensions and total depth, constantly impacting, in the concept of a dignified life, as the highest human right.

In this sense, in addition to expressing a global depression of the economy, it is related to a direct attack on the reproduction of human life itself. The latter, not only has an ethical and humanistic connotation, concerned with ensuring the satisfaction of the basic needs of the population, access to productive resources and subsistence, but also puts in predicament, one of the main sources of wealth social, labor force and nature as a whole. Seen in perspective, the current crisis can be defined as systemic, because it affects the capitalist system as a whole.

It is structural, because it is expressed in multiple dimensions and levels, and is civilizing, because it violates the process of social metabolism, man-nature and places at a crossroads, the foundations of the value and meaning of human civilization.

However, no mechanical solutions can be expected, which envisage the end of capitalism and the automatic passage to a new society, or more modestly, the end of neoliberalism and the triumph of the excluded sectors, but it warns, about the inescapable fact, of that despite its size and depth, the crisis finds more outlets and greater effectiveness in the short term, within the capitalist building itself.

This assumption is valid for the countries in which neocapitalism is implanted and which show a certain response capacity. International capital, which amalgamates the great transnational monopolies and oligopolies, the central and peripheral states, international organizations and the media, among other important actors. On the other hand, the classes, movements and complementary actors appear disintegrated and lack an immediate alternative project, or at least, difficult to assume by the total social collective.

The necessary response would point to structural, systemic and civilizatory change, that is, in a posneoliberal and post-capitalist pattern, but there is no social force to materialize it, and much less, immediately. An important point to take into account in the analysis, lies in the fact that the aforementioned complexity of the crisis manages to be covered up, at least provisionally, by the great setback, which means the global economic depression.

To go beyond mere appearance, it is essential then, to adopt a historical, structural and also strategic perspective. In addition to the economic depression, which reveals a crisis of widespread valorization, the current situation of global implosion must be stated in the plural, such as crises, or the convergence of the various types of breaks, since the global disaster has a disfigured multidimensional face.

In addition to its financial and depressive components, the civilizatory crisis has, at least, nine equally dark faces. The lack of work, not only of the underdeveloped countries, which as a whole, lose labor sovereignty, that is, the capacity to generate sufficient formal employment and quality, demanded above all by the working-age population. The ILO - International Labor Organization- estimates that at the end of in the year **2009**, there were approximately **239** million unemployed people in the world. The food crisis, has been caused by the imbalance of the global agro-food order, which puts the interests of transnational corporations before it, dismantles the production systems of the underdeveloped countries and the peasant way of life, conforming the problem of the loss of sovereignty food and social unsustainability. FAO -Organization for Food and Agriculture- in its **2009** report, estimates that more than a billion people are on the verge of death due to hunger.

Closely linked to the previous one, the risk of subsistence appears. According to figures from the same organization, within the poverty range, there were 4,750 million people in the world, almost ¾ of the world population. Likewise, more than 2,800 million people in the world survive on less than $ **2** per day and **1,200** million people survive, with $ **1** or less per day. Similarly, the UN estimates that at least **150,000** people a day die in the world, because of extreme poverty.

Previously, we have repeatedly, but never sufficiently, referred to environmental deterioration. The disproportion in the consumption of natural resources, in the world capitalist system, is totally unequal, so that **20 %** of the world population, concentrated in the central countries of the north, consumes **80 %** of natural resources. The voracious dynamic of accumulation destroys what nature takes millions of years to build.

The failure in energy sources, is mainly caused by the oligopolistic control of consumer markets, and converts energy resources into a volatile commodity, exposed to speculative attacks, which punish, above all, the underdeveloped countries dependent on energy products, either because they specialize in their production and export or because, lacking them, they depend on their importation. Several analysts announce the end of the era of cheap oil: only **14** of the **54** oil producing countries are still increasing the extraction of crude oil.

The migratory hegira, reaches considerable proportions. Huge contingents of population are heading south-north and the volume of cash remittances, which they send to their countries of origin, has experienced unprecedented growth throughout the world. The volume of emigration has exceeded twice its magnitude in the last 25 years, reaching a historical record of 190 million individuals in the year **2005**. There are no updated data from **2007**, but the trend, marks levels that can be unaffordable. An increasing proportion of these emigrants flee from pressures of labor origin, food shortages and, even more, from the risk of death in war zones.

The political perversion rests on a scaffolding of transnational power, which brings together transnational corporations, imperial states, international organizations and political parties around neoliberalism. However, today there is an institutional crisis, seen as a loss of legitimacy of the neoliberal, state and financial institutions. However, the concentration of power has had such a strong impact that it has dismantled projects and slowed down the path of political agents, who could embody the alternative and social change. At present, there does not seem to be a collective agent, an alternative to big capital and its interests.

Finally, the cultural disorientation, focused on the generation of social knowledge, faces a moment of lethargy, before the imposition of the weight of unique thought and the diffusion of post-structuralism. Likewise, the adoption of micro-social, disconnected and descontextualized analytical frameworks arises from the institutions. As a result, an epistemological break occurs between the macro and the micro, structure and subject, the global plane and local essences and the temporal horizons, the long and the short term. Faced with the worsening of social inequalities, a feeling of discouragement and apathy predominates, and to a lesser extent, resistance and rebellion. Culture is minimized, as a space for criticism, creation and education, to reduce it to its minimum expression, as a mere banal entertainment and absolute contempt for generalized disinformation.

It seems naive then, to review the moral section of the neoliberal macro-system. It simply does not exist, or rather, has suffered an intellectual accommodation, aimed at the justification, no longer, of the performance of the ruling elites, but to a pretended and inexcusable evasion of moral responsibility, by adjusting the utilitarian ethic , to the heavy logic of a failed system. We consciously renounce the details of the fallacies and conceptual and methodological errors committed, assumed and defended by the neoliberal ideology.

They would necessarily lead us to issues that despite their age, become relevant, due to what some theorists have called 'bad development'. They are the subject of another book, due to its significance and extension. The implicit question, about the value of a human life, can not be answered simply by a mention, however broad it may be.

The proposed solutions section, through some well-known social critics, is plagued with micro-utopias or candid and romantic recipes. The return to the community and the development of conviviality, are some examples. They represent the example of euphemistic language, which they criticize outrageously.

Likewise, deglobalization and regionalization are partial and delayed alternatives in the timeline, which draws a suffocating picture, for an exaggerated population volume. Even so, alternatives arise such as the ALBA project, which brings together different South American countries, all led by liberal governments, left or center-left, which seek to achieve a different reintegration in the global, their respective nations, and the global economy.

Another initiative has been offered in the so-called Washington preconsensus, or the theoretical alternative of the "third way". It seems an insurmountable paradox, that the same system that has generated the situation, proposes the solution. The euphemisms issued by the established system are unparalleled and, even less, possible defense. The liberal theorists themselves have described the current system as "creative destruction" and immigration because of the lack of employment opportunities, such as "external labor mobility". Incredible and insufferable, the continued consideration of the social collective, of the people, as a generic entity, intellectually disabled.

Nationalism emerge as an alternative of coexistence. Work continues on increasing urban sustainability, with acceptable progress by large cities, in different aspects, such as public transport or environmental pollution, under the golden rule of sustainable development: "Think globally, act locally". All this in order to preserve the biotic environment and also the abiotic one.

Chapter XIX. A Fiction Genre

> "Whoever puts his hand on me to govern me is a usurper and a tyrant and I declare him my enemy"
>
> -Pierre Joseph Proudhon. French philosopher-

One of the most notable reactions to the results of coercive policies, inspired by neoliberal ideology and, therefore, restrictive policies of governmental origin, as, above all, the practices of savage capitalism, has shaped a dynamic and current of opposition, called by specialists and media, as 'conspiracy theories'.

The most radical version of this current, attributed to ancient secret societies, an objective of world domination and responsibility for major historical events, representative of social and economic evolution, all for teleological purposes, either finalists, religious or pseudo-religious. They vary, yes, the supposed hermetic societies, responsible for such events.

Among them and the best known and notorious, are the Priory of Sion, the Illuminati and the Freemasons. Recently, the presence of former members of these societies has been combined into new groups, notably the Bildelberg Group and the so-called ´300 Committee´.

The Davos Forum has also received significant mentions, as well as the Club of Rome, without being able to include both, strictly speaking, in the category of hermetic societies, although they do show a clear restricted feature and also, restrictive.

The Bildelberg Club is named after the Dutch hotel, where its first meeting took place. The implementation of the Marshall Plan had produced a strong anti-American sentiment in Europe. A Polish politician, Joseph Retinger, together with Prince Bernardo of the Netherlands, promotes a movement, funded by David Rockefeller, destined to face the strengthened communism. All this, in the year **1954**.

It was decided to internationalize the movement, inviting influential people in the international arena, with the intention of discussing political issues, relevant at all times. The meetings were attended by well-known figures, such as Russian President Vladimir Putin, former Spanish President José Luis Rodríguez Zapatero, Queen Sofía of Spain, Prisa Group Executive President Juan Luis Cebrián, and a long list of personalities of politics, business, media and banking. The meetings usually have a variable periodicity, although usually they meet annually. The contents of the meetings are secret and no person is allowed to enter without an invitation.

The same thing does not happen with the *'300 Committee'*. It seems that it originated in the founding of the British East India Company. Directed by Queen Elisabeth Windsor II and the Order of the Garter, it includes among its components, the British Royal Institute of Foreign Affairs, the Tavistock Institute for Human Relations, the Club of Rome, the UN, the US Federal Reserve and certain members of the European high bourgeoisie.

His obsession, like all the groups included in the conspiracy theories, is directed towards the creation of a world government, with absolute control of the citizens and the elimination of the poor majority of the population, which consumes necessary resources, the elimination of religions and popular sovereignty and any imaginable objective. With this group, the conspiracy paranoia, shoots up to reach delirious levels.

The Committee includes the old European bourgeois families, the Illuminati, the American Masonic Order, Skull & Bones, the Church, the Sages of Sion and the International Monetary Fund. Of course, I could not miss the CIA. Apparently, nobody is left out. They are attributed, participation in the death of Pope John Paul I, the assassination of John Fiztgerald Kennedy and influence in the two world wars.

The Official Gazette of the French Republic, includes the creation of the Priory of Sion, in the month of July **1956.** Its intended origins go back to the city of Jerusalem, in the year **1099**, in which on the Mount of Sion, Godfrey of Bouillon, establishes a secret lineage belonging to the Merovingian dynasty. Its origins, join the Knights Templar and apparently, after an itinerary based in Sicily, in **1627**, ended up joining the Jesuit order. Its initial purpose, seemed to be in the protection of the line of genetic descent of Jesus of Nazareth. We believe that the greatest beneficiary of its existence has been for the author Dan Brown, with the publication of his literary work, then taken to the cinema, The Da Vinci Code.

A very different case is represented by the ´Illuminati of Bavaria Order´. The organization was founded at the time of the French Enlightenment. As its name suggests, its components were educated and educated people, some advanced for their time. Among its objectives were the struggle against the power of the state or the demand for equal rights between the sexes. With the support of the ruling State of Bavaria, the Catholic Church, banned society in the year **1785**. As in the previous cases, has been attributed the goal of global control.

The most balanced positions of conspiracy theory progress continuously and at an accelerated rate. They are grouped into public acts and documents, social platforms, conferences, movements and organizations. It is surprising, the level of detail and accuracy of the published information.

These criticisms are directed towards a large number of facts, always extreme initiative in the causation of situations and very diverse phenomena. The active participation of the American Intelligence Center -CIA- is one of the constants of the conspiracy story.

Two axes on the others, dominate the criticism and analysis of conspiracy theories. Basically, the control of the world population and its means to obtain it and the excessive desire to accumulate wealth. In the second chapter, as an initial step, the focus has been placed on the use of the arms industry. In fact, after the Second World War, more than **200** armed, regional and local conflicts have been recorded. In no case, the participating factions, either regions, political factions or small countries, had the capacity to manufacture armaments.

The arms industry of the developed western countries has supplied the weapons, which after the conflicts for which they were initially destined, have ended up in the hands of the terrorist groups, which the political class says they want to fight.

The second rung of the global business, is the reconstruction of the countries that the war has destroyed. The large construction companies perform mammoth works, including costly national infrastructures. Probably, the arms manufacturing and construction corporations belong to the same financial group or to a client or friend group. A delicate point, which conspiracy theories place in the same angle, lies in the elimination of any obstacle that hinders the business objective, leading to the elimination of socially relevant persons.

The Kennedy brothers and the Swedish Prime Minister, Olof Palme, are two clear examples. The anti-war positions of the three politicians and their pacifist attitude, would have signed their death sentence, at the hands of more or less explicit macro-operations. In the case of John F. Kennedy, it seems to be appreciated, a remarkable level of relaxation of security measures, given the high probability of an attack on his life.

The case of the Swedish president seems simpler, although uncertainty persists, about the physical authorship of the assassination. In this line of absence of morality of the dominant elites, a defender of the conspiracy, quotes a textual phrase from a member of the financial elite in this regard: "Iraq has turned out better than we expected."

The role of international banking in corruption, money laundering and intermediation in the purchase of weapons is illustrative. The illegal drug trafficking market, according to unofficial data, constitutes the largest volume of illicit profits and money, at a planetary level. An economic amount of such magnitude, has no possibility of being laundered, without the conscious participation and support of large international banks, some located in the very center of Europe.

The design of real distortions of financial engineering, in combination with specialized law firms, is dedicated to this task, normally using screen companies based in tax havens, through 'offshore' accounts. In the arms business, according to conspiracy theories, banks abandon their role of intermediation and advice, to become capitalist partners and active accomplices. Its objective lies in the construction of new debt by revolutionaries and insurgents, sometimes from established governments.

Unfortunately, international justice as part of the system, is limited to the containment of this phenomenon, from a multitude of trenches. Justice, paradoxically, is the object of friendly fire, as well as an enemy.

In the section on the achievement of world sovereignty, documents multiply. The search for a world government is the most important statement, without a doubt. This dreamlike purpose is achieved in several ways. Through the use of ancient and metaphysical techniques and powers, by economic influence or by the control of the mass media of social communication.

Technology offers greater progressive control, to the point of total vigilance, the big global brother, capable of controlling movements and thoughts. The possibility always exists. On the other hand, the laws of probability are reluctant to the fact that a determined group, however powerful it may be, is capable of influencing the two world wars, the escalation to Hitler's power and the financing of movements and counter-global movements.

Chapter XX. A Happy Ending?

> "Only one thing makes a dream impossible: the fear of failing."
>
> - Paulo Coelho, Brazilian writer-

The background of the problem of an unequal society really consists in the fact that the neoliberal creed has been established as a popular ideology. Eduardo Galeano, expressed in an informal talk on television, that "you can not imprison who has the keys of the jail." He also stated that the Berlin Wall has been replaced by the fences of Ceuta -Africa- or the borders of Syria -Middle East-.

The International Observatory of Human Rights, warns that the dictatorship is the enemy of dignity. Left intellectuals enact slogans that sound good, but are unable to accompany them with the appropriate musical band. Grandiloquent sentences such as "the revolution is necessary, since the reform does not work", "only the overthrow of the established power is valid" or "we must reconquer the symbolic mentality". They are mere sentences, using formulas of normative language that express desires or utopias. The same kind of language they say to despise.

The problem goes beyond that. It is not even, unfortunately, only the suffering and massacre of the poor and disinherited, of those who have assumed poverty as a stigma. It is, above all, that the global socioeconomic system has become a chaotic system. The governance of such a system is simply not feasible.

This, along with other issues of political philosophy and social engineering, will be addressed in our third installment, about an equally developed society. This is so, since there is a general agreement among most social systems specialists, around the question of the possibility of designing a social system, equitable, balanced, inter-generationally responsible, factually possible and above all, necessary. Social design is possible, even based on mathematical equations. All in all, its orientation and philosophy must be taken and materialized in an idea that quickly gains acceptance: social inclusion.

This rule is generalizable, desirable and indispensable, for social institutions. As an illustration of the different roads, which can lead to an identical destination, two men appear habitually, among the greatest world fortunes according to Forbes magazine. They are Carlos Slim and Bill Gates. They represent, two opposites in the ways of achieving wealth. The first, through the typical methods of neocapitalism.

Clientelist relations, permissiveness in opaque businesses, fiscal impunity. The second, by virtue of a business-oriented society, with social institutions designed for that same purpose and an ideology, that favor support for the business mentality, curiously, in the country that most likely represents the highest level of corruption of the western world. But it has favored coherent individual initiative, in some cases, and above all, has been able to exercise constant self-criticism, from its powerful and influential public opinion. Oliver Stone or the reporters denouncing the Watergate case, Carl Bernstein and Bob Woodward, are cases that deserve to be remembered.

The concept and the repeated use of the term crisis, by governments, as an indefensible justification, of cutting or coercive measures, in economic terms or of social freedoms, offends intelligence, with the same intensity, with which it annoys the senses. Crisis of democracy, crisis of the state, crisis of values, crisis of the welfare state.

It is a typical case, in which the repetition, provides credibility, scares, inhibits and inhibits, and even worse, pushes acceptance and its most disastrous consequence, inaction.

Polyarchy, or better yet, Polyarchy universalization, is seen on the horizon as a small but visible brightness, to pursue, to work. Its real meaning depends on the density and conceptual and social weight that the citizenship is capable of granting, of the substantiality of its implementation. Its meaning, similar to the 'co-management' used in the workplace, in past decades, directly refers to the 'power match'.

It is not about sharing government management; that measure borders on the factual impossibility. It is about the consideration, on the part of the institutional managers, beginning with their maximum executive power, of the consideration of the opinion and positions of the relevant social actors. We are again witnessing the incredible paradox that the resolutions voted by a majority in the parliament of the Spanish nation, the highest elected representative of popular sovereignty, are not converted into laws or legal provisions by the government.

In any case, we do not share, the general belief, that the revolutionaries were all brave, but necessary. The acceptance by the formal governments of the different countries, of the weight and necessary participation of the relevant organizations and social groups, must be handled as an instrumental way, a vexed and despised process: the agreement by negotiation and social consensus.

The 'trans' and 'post' prefixes are repeated in the same way, constantly, in order to define at the same time, the desire to overcome a nefarious period for the social group, as well as access to a new era, necessarily higher quality and progress. The trans or postcapitalism is a clear example. Similarly, postmodernism, evidence, progress and improvement of the modern age, whose end, many historians, place in World War II, as a terminal point.

It is essential to adopt a systemic perspective and a panoramic view, with perspective, of the facts presented here. It should be considered that the essence of the global system consists in the unfolding of the concepts of power and authority, which should conform, a single element of cultural and social leadership.

However, dualism has reoccurred. The real power is held by a part of the system that is illegitimate, as far as authority is concerned, the global financial elites have the power. The authority, legitimately granted by the people, is concentrated in the State, represented in its executive branch by governments. For that reason, the political perception of society longs for a charismatic leader.

The leader unites both powers. He has authority and exercises power. It is the secret of the triumph of the great revolutionaries and the reason for their popular veneration. And also the reason that their power has been transformed into dictatorships of both political signs.

Another cause, already repeated at the moment, of the current deteriorated situation, consists of social myopia, induced by the strategies of fear and coercion. The existence of fictitious enemies, which haunt the social system as a whole, can be called communism or terrorism, but they perfectly serve their purpose. The perspectives of uncertainty generated in the average citizen, are by their very nature, constitutive of threats, morally and materially unbearable. The human being, needs assurances and certainties.

Without losing perspective, we have observed how there are countries that are outside the direct sphere of global power, at least in part. Without exception, these social spaces are supported by a cultural system, different qualitatively. The prevailing social values are oriented towards an equality of their societies, derived from the implantation in their reference values, of groups and individuals.

The direct solution, then, goes through the creation of a renewed cultural system. We have affirmed, that any objective, necessarily implies, a process and one of the necessary components of it, is the time horizon. The renewal of the social system, or else, the break with the previous paradigmatic framework, must necessarily be measured in representative units of generations. It is accepted, as an estimated unit of measurement, that a generation is approximately equivalent to 25 calendar years. A social transformation, of the nature of the one suggested here, will behave at least one generation and, more likely, two.

The constitutive parameters of a culture are unquestionably based on education, understood as a formative process, continent of social values, as well as of scientific, academic and relational or affective competences. Even the former British Prime Minister, Tony Blair, unconditional ally of American imperialism, pronounced as a mantra for the global future: "education, education, education." The maximum value must continue necessarily climbing the individual freedom, but as a component of a greater system, materialized in the community. In a second large package, there are legal and regulatory provisions.

The values of justice and social equity, together with the decision-making capacity of individuals, to guide the beacon of legal legislation, must be the means and end, form and substance of the total process. Finally, the supreme values of both sources of general information and authority, - legal system and educational system- must coincide.

They can serve perfectly, those principles, collected in almost all Western national constitutions and different declarations of human rights. It can be reflected graphically.

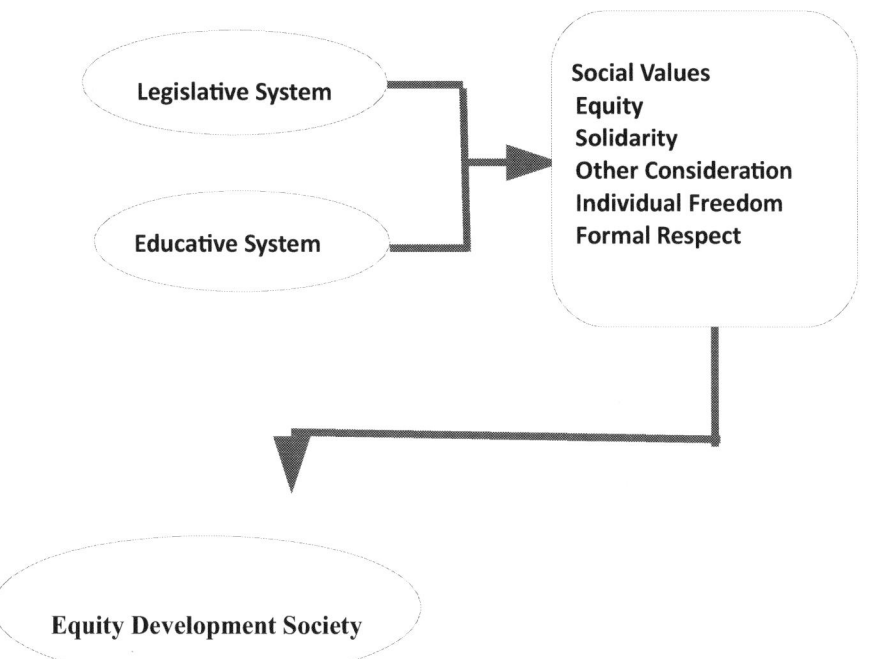

Minimum indispensable components for the configuration of a value system as an indispensable basis of an equitable and advanced social system.

With the aim of facilitating an already established guideline, the Scandinavian model of orientation and social democratic base, stands as a model to follow. It would facilitate the attainment of the great objective of economic growth, as well as the continuation of basic research and the impulse of technological development, inherent in human evolution.

A public policy of support and development of individual initiatives and innovations, with greater emphasis on those that favor the development of the social collective, that is, that can be applied for the general benefit, would constitute a safe format and probably with positively unexpected results. in terms of quantity and number of results achieved. It is a simple rule. The use as a general principle of action, of the most perfect existing machine, that nature has taken millions of years to give us: the human brain. From the traditional political point of view, the coincidence in the diagnostic phase of the problem of the global society seems to be overcome and with more than unanimous character.

The second phase, the generation of alternatives, registers proposals, coming from varied, sufficient and promising disciplines. From the *'third way'*, advocated among others, by sociologists like Giddens and defended later by relevant sociologists like Toffler, to the new polyarchy, a concept that entails annex, a higher level of social participation. The basic problem remains rooted in the subject and the way, that is, in whom and how.

Political parties are part of the problem, more than the solution and can not lead a change of such magnitude. The use of the most advanced existing machine, the human brain and the promotion and use of the innovative ideas provided by the innovative individual, find different obstacles for its widespread use. From the lack of social habit, through the public and private support of new ideas, to the opposition of large industrial corporations.

All this, without counting on the already known resistance to change, negative bulwark, strongly established in traditional societies. However, there are valid initiatives and very commendable, exciting beginnings of the way forward, in local Spanish governments. The social innovation agency that the Basque government has developed in our country deserves to be highlighted as an innovative alternative in participation and social support.

Epilogue

Dependencies, due favors, promises of exclusive belonging, promotions, support for an uncertain future, help to an acquaintance's friend, concessions to the future. Generalized transfers on the individual level but more illegitimate, the more power granted by the people is held. The members of the coercive class need the exclusive circles and societies to self-reinforce and stimulate their lack of moral behavior.

Even with everything, issues and partial initiatives are registered. Do we need leadership? This has been historically, although perhaps socially disturbing. Attempts to attack the medium, the instrument, specifically, money, such as bitcoin. We found no solution other than education and it is a measure, with medium-term results. We sincerely doubt that adequate legislation essentially modifies the typical behavior of power.

But we need more subjects and fewer objects, more motivation than false illusion, the prohibition of roads already traveled, if not the assault to the skies, yes the boarding to a limbo with free access, as a platform of new impulse; the desire that the common and not exclusive, becomes the landscape that provides enjoyment and welfare accessible to the social majority.

The global system has become chaotic. It has generated the entrance into panic, the paranoid schizophrenia of the neo-capitalist system, due to the appearance of one of the phantasmagorical figures most feared by any power, although historically and culturally desirable, unavoidable, that terrifies the dreams of the elites, flooding them with constant nightmares and repetitive: the loss of control, in large part, due to the evolution of new communication technologies and the persistent progression of technological innovation.

In the schizophrenic paroxysm, produced by that same terror, the powerful international capitalism, tries its desperate braces, exhales its last breaths for survival, international agreements that evade any kind of legal arbitration, the institutionalization of corruption, through the persistent search for that perhaps, it represents the greatest and oldest longing of neoliberal thought: the privatization of the State itself.

The chosen formula, the golden retirement, the glazed moral cage, the anticipation of the reward for complicity, to the current political leaders, in the structure of the organisms that generate capital accumulation par excellence: the big industrial corporations.

This phenomenon has been labeled by politicians and the media as "revolving doors". The future retribution in exchange for the current favor. This practice, should be noted, that generalized globally, of neoliberal behavior, has received by political parties and media, a successful label 'governments in the shade'. Thus, another new paradox emerges in the panorama.

It is probabilistically safer, belonging to a notorious financial group, to stand for democratic elections, if it is to display political power and social influence. Money turns dreams into reality, also and perhaps above all, the delusions of greatness.

The watchtower of power of the elites, magnificently defined by Sloterdinj, through the metaphor of the 'golden sphere', is shaken by the growing and deep reactions of the despised world collectivity. The slave labor of children, manufacturing sports and fashion products, enslaved producers of subsidiary companies of multinationals, who wash away the intrinsic sin of human exploitation, by placing a friendly logo and excellently resolved graphically. The families without minimum rights, the abusive conditions of the bank evictions, the laws of coasts, promulgated to the measure of the interests of the constructors, the indiscriminate industrial pollution; they are some dynamiting examples of the reaction of the social collective, despised, beaten and subdued.

Systems theory calls frozen events a series of determining events in the past that condition the current situation and whose modification is costly or very improbable. This is the big question. This is, exactly the case of the birth of the current neoliberalism, with the great world agreement of Bretton Woods; the birth of savage hegemonic capitalism. In this same systemic current, Ilia Prigogine, was awarded the Nobel Prize, for its concept of *'dissipative structures'* of a system, but also contributed, the necessary idea of *'nucleación'*, of which many theorists and scholars, seem to forget. The planetary economic system generates more disorder than stability. The existence of a nucleus, formed by the great international capitalism, dominates and determines the total system.

But it generates excessive turbulence in the world system. A multitude of dissipative structures have emerged, through which to channel dissatisfaction, protest and global resistance.

Social networks, non-governmental organizations, specific associations and some political parties are some examples. An observation, using a wide angle, can affirm with tranquility, that the opposition to the globalizing economic system has developed and turned into a solid and growing trend. The peaceful protests in each of the Davos forums are a clear example.

The great paradox, not assumed by the existing economic power, lies in the fact that the systemic inequality and the policies of cuts that imply are totally ineffective in the only area of interest of neoliberalism: the economic area. Restriction slows growth. Is it possible, a change of social model in the sense of greater social equity? Will the action led by a leader be required? The answer is clear and objectively affirmative. Science and history confirm this. Mahatma Gandhi, Martin Luther King, Nelson Mandela and in his own way, John F. Kennedy, went down that road, seeking the same end. Peace and equality, they have formalized the utopically intended objectives.

If the dissipative structure is defined, as a channel through which to eliminate the tension of a certain system, social networks have become an authentic 'global therapist'. The demonstrations of the outraged groups find an audience and a response panel, of dimensions never before imagined. A new variable of the system, which political parties and business corporations, strive to dominate.

The approach of the essential questions, in the public and common plane, to glimpse the probability of chance in the future, the solution of technical paradoxes and social expositions, leads us to a new delivery, and at the end of the series, that tries to anticipate the future.

Partial solutions are ineffective and inappropriate. Although the accumulation of capital, is presented as one of the faces of the multi-causal determinant of the current situation, money, as a visible instrument, is not the real problem. The bitcoin and the local currencies, as alternatives, become mere anecdotes. The global system, requires new ingredients -components- in order, to achieve the desired and necessary, state of calm and balance. An effort to anticipate the future, which will be marked both by voluntarist human action and by chance.

Two entelechies, without any real counterpoint, credit and debt, have become the beacons, which guide the dark world economic landscape. In relation to this point, it is worth highlighting the need to escape from the reductionist and disqualifying nominalisms and labels used in the neoliberal political discourse usually.

They are heard, expressed with absolute ignorance and contempt, qualifying as 'popular' and 'radical', to define ideological positions, contrary to the practices dictated by the established power. No group or social alternative, is positioned against wealth.

On the contrary, they oppose poverty. The signs of ostentation of the great fortunes, can be considered a comparative grievance, but in any case, depends on the individual moral, its use and exposure. However, they should be taxed equally, by the institutional authority, through a tax rate, intended to contribute to the general welfare. The fortunes are not obtained in a vacuum, but, necessarily, in the social environment.

The logic, not only economic, indicates that the business initiative is not only licit, but also necessary. In a world dominated by the economy, another alternative, of a radical or softened meaning, would constitute a suicide, or rather, a magnicide. Another question is the determination of the mode and limits of the economic methodology. It must necessarily be differentiated between the realities arising from high profits and excessive accumulation.

During our presentation, a repeated reference to the concept of system has taken place. The theory of complex systems provides explanatory parameters of the national situation and also worldwide. The system transcends individuals. It self-feeds itself and shows a marked tendency toward self-organization. In our country, only as an example of the tendency towards systemic perfection, the Punic plot has been perfected with respect to its predecessor, the Gürtel plot.

The corruption system has become sophisticated. Consequently, the importance of the temporal dimension in the social process can be understood. Immediate solutions are needed, beginning necessarily, by partial remedies. The results reacts, once again, to the law of exponential growth.

Surely, in our country, one more legislature, of the only party prosecuted for corruption in democratic history, will not contribute to the eradication of the game of corrupt exchanges of capital and public goods, nor will it do so at the global level, the election of a president of the power with greater imperialist anxiety, of marked fascist orientation.

A change of paradigm is needed, in the sense used by Khun. A surgical process of extirpation, of the neoliberal values and also, the substitution of old dominating concepts, in the socioeconomic formalization. Responsibility replacing blame, conviction reinforcing solidarity, everyday support diversity, the abandonment of competition replaced by collaboration and above all, peace and global stability as a philosophy and vital mantra.

In this line, the conclusions drawn from the progress in the study of dynamic systems far from equilibrium, do not offer promising prospects. The social structure, is defined in reality, as a complex system of deep relationships. In that sense, it is subject, like the rest of the networks, to the appearance and imperative of the "power laws". Specifically, in the economic sphere, the continuous repetition of prevailing practices in the world market, have originated a 'vicious circle', so that the most favored minority, will continue to accumulate wealth, to the detriment of the large minority increasingly impoverished.

This fact has been called *'San Mateo principle'*, due to the text of the evangelist, who in chapter **13**, verse **12**, says: "Because whoever has, will be given more and will abound; and whoever does not have, even what he has, will be taken from him."Matthew [13,12] Also, in San Marcos-chapter **4,** verse **25**-and in Luke-chapters **8** and **19,** vers. **18** and **26**-, the same idea is repeated The world economic system continues to illustrate the maximum representation of a zero-sum game, so that a few win, most must lose, away from the scheme of all win, typical of the theory of the games, as for example, the prisoner's dilemma.

Bauman suggests that as a complex system, organized social reactions should lead to a re-normalization of the social set, as historically, they have been the Bolshevik revolution, May 68, universal suffrage and other examples. But this possibility of influence of any part of the system on another, happens when both parties are interconnected. The separation between rich and poor, is total, qualitative. The elites can not be influenced by the reaction of the majorities. They belong to different worlds, qualitatively different spheres.

The English current of the sciences of the complexity, contributes another data. The complex systems, among them, the social set, are only susceptible of a partial arrangement -POSET, partially ordered sets, in their Castilian translation-. Among other reasons, because problems arise, denominated in unspeakable orthodox logic and in complex sociology, intractable situations. This means that although the problems are clearly identified and theoretical solutions are found, the cost of their practical and real solution are unacceptable due to their magnitude. Current examples are the international financial system, global warming, hunger and poverty or pollution of the oceans.

The psychological sensation that is breathed, shows such a degree of negativity, that a concept emerged as a consequence of the theory of catastrophes, proposed by Thom in the decade of the **70's**, takes more and more influence and is outlined with greater clarity. Its about *'collapse'*, in this case, *'civilizing'*.

Just as a biological organism, a social or civilizational system, collapses when several systems fail simultaneously. In our case, politics has become the legitimization of a form of property, exclusive of neoliberal practice and law has derived legislative, has transmuted into the grammar of social inequality, ie, the political text. As a positive alternative, the idea of a new civilization arises, either on our planet or outside it, or even in parallel.

However, observing the Scandinavian social democracy, one can think of the real option of achieving certain standards of social equity, even when the scientific principles derived from the sciences of complexity indicate the negation of that fact. Are we facing an inconsistency between theory and social practice? Absolutely not. The 'social values' make up the pillars on which the building of culture is based. In terms used by Naruyama, culture is the authentic *'mental landscape'* -mindscape- the decisive conceptual category that feeds a definite social system, definitely complex. An abstraction that governs the real behavior of the individual in society.

In any case, it requires the birth of a new society, of a modified landscape, necessarily and whatever the means, either by implosion or by own decision; a new model of society, here on our planet or outside of it, or more likely, in both places at the same time, in parallel, over a long time horizon. A society with such profound changes, that they will become an authentic human metamorphosis. ¿An immortal society?

Sources and References

Conferences

Caputo, O."La crisis actual de la economía mundial. Una nueva Interpretación teórica e histórica", ponencia presentada en XII Seminario Internacional Los partidos y una nueva sociedad, México, 19-21 de marzo de 2009.

Foladori, G. "Las nanotecnología en el contexto actual", ponencia presentada en el foro Nanotecnología en México: oportunidades y retos de la actualidad, Zacatecas, México, 24 de septiembre, 2009.

Grimalt, P. Caos Determinístico. Conferencia. 24-IV-1996. Ciclo *Creatividad y Caos. Valencia,* Universidad Politécnica.

Savater, F. Valores Éticos en la Estructura de la Sociedad Civil. Conferencia pronunciada en el Centro Cultural Bancaja. Ciclo Conferencias en el Centro. Valencia, 11-VI-1992.

Vasapollo, L. "La precariedad como paradigma de la reestructuración capitalista en la fase de la crisis estructural", ponencia presentada en las XI Jornadas de Economía Crítica, Bilbao, 27-29 de marzo, 2008.

Internet

FAO(2009), "El número de víctimas del hambre es mayor que nunca",en http://www.fao.org/fileadmin/user_upload/newsroom/docs/Press%20release%20june-es.pdf.

Petras,J (2005), "Seis mitos sobre los beneficios de la inversión extranjera", Rebelión, en http://www.rebelion.org/noticias/2005/7/1742.pdf.

Idem (2009), "Depresión mundial, guerras regionales y declive del imperio de EEUU", Rebelión, en http://www.rebelion.org/noticia.php?id=83718

Quesada. A. "Complejidad y Comportamiento Humano". Édition électronique: http://polis.reveu.org

Tagliavini, A. ElFuturo dela Esperanza. 3ª Edición. http://www.eumed.net/libros-gratis/20014/1938/index.htm

Press

Newspapers and magazines

Bartra, A. , "La gran crisis",La Jornada. 10 de marzo de2009.

Bello,W."Todo lo que usted quería saber sobre el origen de esta crisis pero teme no entenderlo", Focus on the Golobal South, 2008.

Brunner, J.J. "Investigación social y decisiones políticas: El mercado del conocimiento".Nueva Sociedad Nº 146 Noviembre-Diciembre 1996, pp.108-121.

Chaparro Guevara, G. "No Linealidad, Complejidad y Sistemas Sociales". antropol.sociol. No. 10, Enero - Diciembre 2008, págs. 197 –219.

Ciencia, la computación afectiva. Diario El País,13/05/2016

Delgado Wise, Raúl y Márquez, H. "Towards a New Theoretical Approach to Understanding the Relationship between Migration and Development" en SocialAnalysis, Specialissue,2009.

Del Refugio, M.,Vázquez,S. &Romo,P.I. . "La emociones y masas. Un resurgimiento de los movimientos sociales masivos". Sphera Publica, 2, (16), 73-91,2016.

Editorial. El Universal, 29 de mayo de 2009.

Holtz-Giménez, E. "Cinco mitos sobre agrocombustibles", Le Monde Diplomatique, edición Cono Sur, núm. 96, 2007.

Katz, C. "Codicia, regulación o capitalismo", Herramienta, núm. 41.

Márquez, H. "México en vilo: desmantelamiento de la soberanía laboral y dependencia de las remesas", Papeles de población, vol. 14, núm. 58, 2009.

Idem "La gran crisis del capitalismo neoliberal", Documentos de trabajo, Unidad Académica en Estudios del Desarrollo, UAZ, 2009a.

Idem. "Hacia la construcción de los estudios críticos del desarrollo", Documentos de trabajo, Unidad Académica en Estudios del Desarrollo, UAZ, 2009b.

Mora, H. "¿Divergencia internacional o desarrollo desigual? Ensayo sobre los fundamentos del comercio internacional, la condición periférica y el subdesarrollo", Revisa Aportes, núm. 1, 2009.

Orgaz, L.,Molina, L.y Carrasco, C."El Creciente Peso de las Economías Emergentes en la Economía y Gobernanza Mundiales. Los Países Bric".Documentos Ocasionales N.º 1101.
Banco de España. Eurosistema.

Riádigos, C. y Martins Esteves, M.S. "Democracia basada en la equidad y en la autogestión: algunas expresiones sociales y educativas" en Educação em Perspectiva, Viçosa,v.7, n. 2, p. 346-366, jul.2016.

Tarride,M. "Complexity and Complex Systems".Mahuinhos II/(1): 46-66. Mar-Jun, 1995

Television

Galeano, E. El orden criminal del mundo. Programa "En Portada". RTVE, Madrid, 13-10-2012.

Nair, S. E. Entrevista en programa "Millennium".RTVE,08/11/2016.

Nair ,S. Entrevista.
internacional.elpais.com/internacional/2002/03/26/.

Sábato,E. Programa "En Portada".RTVE, Madrid,2006.

Books

Acemoglou, D. y Robinson, J.A. Por qué Fracasan Los Países. Los Orígenes del Poder, la Prosperidad y la Pobreza. Editorial Planeta Colombiana, 2012.

Adolfo de Paz, M. "La Desintegración de las Sociedades". Eumed.net libros. 2014.

Alcántara Sáez, M. "Gobernabilidad: Crisis y Cambio". Fondo Cultura Económica. Mexico, 1995. 2ª Ed.

Amin, S. Las luchas campesinas y obreras frente a los desafíos del siglo XXI, El viejo topo, Barcelona, 2005.

Arrighi, G. Adam Smith en Pekín. Orígenes y fundamentos del siglo XXI, Akal, Madrid, 2007.

Altvater, E. El Precio del Bienestar. Edicions Alfons el Magnànim-IVEI, Valencia, 1994.

Beinstein, J. "La crisis en la era senil del capitalismo. Esperando inútilmente el quinto Kondratiev", en El viejo topo, núm. 253, 2009.

Bootkin, D.B. Armonías Discordantes: Una Ecología para el siglo XXI. Círculo de Lectores, Barcelona, 1996.

Boron, A. "Crisis capitalista y reestructuración internacional: consecuencias para América Latina "Facultad de Ciencia Política y Relaciones Internacionales Universidad Católica de Córdoba. Octubre de 2015

Castells, M. The Corneto Society: A Cross-Cultural Perspective. Northampton,2004, MA: Edward Elgar.

Cammilleri, R. Los Monstruos de la Razón. Ediciones Rialp, Madrid,1995.

CórdobaTorres,J.N. "Estrategias de Comunicación en Medios Tradicionales y No Tradicionales".Universidad Mónica Herrera. Guayaquil,Ecuador,2016.

Dahl, R. "A Preface to Democratic Theory,cap.3".The University of Chicago Press,1956.

Daly,H.E. The perils of FreeTrade. Scientific American, November 1993, pp.50-57.

Daly,H. y Cobb, J.Parael Bien Común. México DF: Fondo de Cultura Económica,1993.

Daumas, M. Las Grandes Etapas del Progreso Técnico. México,FCE,1983.

Durkheim, E. El Suicidio: Estudio de Sociología. Ed. Losada,2004.

Feyerabend,P. Adiós a la razón. EditorialTecnos.Madrid, 1996, p.16-17.

Foreman-Peck, J. "Historia Económica Mundial".Prentice Hall. Madrid,2004.

Georgescu Roegen, N. TheEntropyLaw and the Economic Process. Cambridge:Harvard University Press,1971.

Gödel, K. Obras Completas. Alianza Editorial, Madrid,2006.

Guichon, R.A. "Construyendo preguntasen el camino. Comunidades originarias y cientificas". CONICET,Provincia de Buenos Aires, Argentina, 2016.

Harvey, D."El 'nuevo' imperialismo: acumulación por desposesión", en Panitch, Leo y Colin Leys (eds.), El nuevo desafío imperial. SocialRegister2004, CLACSO, BuenosAires,2005.

Haliday,M.A.K. El Lenguaje como Semiótica Social. Fondo de Cultura de México,20015.

Hanson, V.C. Matanzas y Cultura: Batallas Decisivas en el Auge de la Civilización Occidental. EdicionesTurner,2004.

Hawking, S. Historia del Tiempo. RBA Editores, Barcelona,1993.

Hinkelammert,Franz y Mora,H. Hacia una economía para la vida. Preludio a una reconstrucción de la economía, Editorial Tecnológica de Costa Rica, Cartago,2008.

Igual Luis,D. "La Formación de Élites Económicas: Banqueros, Comerciantes y Empresarios".Universidad de Castilla de la Mancha. Publicación Interna.

Jalife-Rahme, A. Hacia la desglobalización, México, Jorale Editores,2007.

Katz, C. La Economía Marxista Hoy. Maia Ediciones. Autopublicación,2009.

Kuhn,Th.S. L a Estructura del as Revoluciones Científicas. Fondo de Cultura Económica,2000.

Loizaga,P.J.(Dir). Diccionario de Pensadores Modernos. Emecé Editores. Barcelona,1996.

Madruga, A. "Crisis en el x.XXI". Autopublicación.2013

Maldonado,C.E. y Gómez Cruz, N.A. "El mundo de las ciencias de la complejidad: Un estado del arte Documento de Investigación No. 76. Universidad del Rosario. Facultad de Administración Editorial Universidad del Rosario, BogotáD.C.Mayo2010.

Marx,K. El Capital. Crítica de la Economía Política. México DF: Fondo de Cultura Económica, 1999.

Marchioni, A. Civilizaciones Antiguas: Vistas desde el Cielo. Paidós Ibérica, S.A.,2003.

Marx,K. El capital. El Proceso de producción del capital. Tomo I,Vol.2, Siglo XXI Editores,México,1975.

Meadows,D.,Meadows, D.L., Randers, J.&Behrens,W.W.III. The Limits of Growth. Universe, Nueva York,1972.

Monod, J. El Azar y la Necesidad. Barral Editores,
 Barcelona,1972.

Morin, E. El Método (2 vols). Cátedra, Madrid,1993.

Morin, Ed. Introducción al Pensamiento Complejo. Gedisa, Barcelona,1995.

Nisbet, R. Historia de la Idea de Progreso. Gedisa, Barcelona,1996.

Oldroyd,D.ElArcodel Conocimiento. Crítica, Barcelona,1993.

Parés,R. La Revolución Cientifica. Pirámide, Madrid,1987.

Piketty.Th. "Capitalism in Tweenty-First Century". RBA de. Barcelona, 2015.

Pinillos, J. L. En el corazón del Laberinto. Espasa Calpe, Madrid, 1997.

Popper, K. La Lógica de la Investigación Científica. Ed. Tecnos, Madrid, 2008.

Price, D.J.S. Hacia una Ciencia de la Ciencia. Ediciones Ariel, Barcelona, 1973.

Prigogine, I. y Stengers, I. La Nueva Alianza. Círculo de Lectores, Barcelona, 1997.

Rella, F. Metamorfosis. Espasa & Calpe, Madrid, 1989.

Ruiz, R. Historia del Pensamiento Científico. México, 2006.

Samuelson, P. y Nordhaus, W. Economía. Buenos Aires: McGraw – Hill, N.Y, 2003.

Sánchez Ron, J.M. El Poder de la Ciencia. Alianza Editorial, Madrid, 1992.

Sanmartin, J. Tecnología y Futuro Humano. Anthropos. Barcelona, 1990.

Schopenhauer, A. El Dolor del Mundo y el Consuelo de la Religión. Aldebarán eds., 1998.

Schumpeter, S.A. Capitalismo, Socialismo y Democracia (Vol. I). Ediciones Folio, Barcelona, 1996.

Servan-Schreiber, J.J. El Desafío Mundial. Plaza & Janés Editores, Barcelona, 1988.

Solé, R.V. y Otros. Complejidad en la Frontera del Caos. *Investigación y Ciencia*. Mayo, págs. 14-21.

Tamames, R. Introducción a la Economía Internacional. Alianza Editorial, S.A. Madrid, 1983.

Toffler, A. La Tercera Ola. Plaza & Janés, Barcelona, 1980.

Toffler, A. Avances y Premisas. Plaza & Janés, Barcelona, 1983.

Toffler. A. El Shock del Futuro. Plaza & Janés Editores, S.A., Barcelona, 1992.

Touraine, A. Crítica a la Modernidad. Temas de Hoy, Madrid, 1993

Veltmeyer, H." The Global Crisis and Latin America", en Martijn Konings (ed.), Beyond the Subprime Headlines: Critical Perspectives on the Financial Crisis, Verso, Londres, 2009.

Ventós, R. Ensayos sobre el Desorden. Kairós, Barcelona, 1986.

Wallerstein, I. La decadencia del poder estadounidense, Era, México, 2005.

Weber, M. El origen del capitalismo moderno en Historia económica general (1923-24), México, F.C.E., 1978.

Woolgar, S. Ciencia: Abriendo la Caja Negra. Anthropos. Madrid, 1991.

Manufactured by Amazon.ca
Bolton, ON